where I found God today

ENCOUNTERING THE DIVINE IN ORDINARY PLACES

EDITORS OF GUIDEPOSTS

A Gift from Guideposts

Thank you for your purchase! We want to express our gratitude for your support with a special gift just for you.

Dive into *Spirit Lifters*, a complimentary e-book that will fortify your faith, offering solace during challenging moments. Its 31 carefully selected scripture verses will soothe and uplift your soul.

Please use the QR code or go to **guideposts.org/spiritlifters** to download.

Where I Found God Today: Encountering the Divine in Ordinary Places

Published by Guideposts
100 Reserve Road, Suite E200
Danbury, CT 06810
Guideposts.org

Copyright © 2025 by Guideposts. All rights reserved.

This book, or parts thereof, may not be reproduced, stored in a retrieval system, or transmitted in any form or by any means, electronic, mechanical, photocopying, recording, or otherwise, without the written permission of the publisher.

Cover and interior design by Andrew Nahem
Cover photo by Jiang Hongyan/Shutterstock
Typeset by Aptara, Inc.

ISBN (softcover): 978-1-961442-16-0
ISBN (epub): 978-1-961442-17-7

Printed and bound in the United States of America
10 9 8 7 6 5 4 3 2 1

CONTENTS

Introduction 1

1 *Finding God in Little Gifts* 5

2 *Finding God in Guiding Signs* 31

3 *Finding God in Times of Need* 55

4 *Finding God in Connections across Time* 81

5 *Finding God in Messages of Love* 107

6 *Finding God in Nature* 141

7 *Finding God in Loved Ones* 167

8 *Finding God in Ordinary Moments* 191

9 *Finding God in the Home* 223

Devotion Index 248

Author Index 250

INTRODUCTION

Stretching Our Awareness of God

Missy Buchanan

On most days I wake up when it is still dark outside. Instinctively I turn over and fully extend my legs and arms, flexing my stiff muscles as I toss back the covers. Oftentimes I give an audible groan. My aging joints are tight from hours of inactivity, so I sit up on the side of the bed, arch my back and do a few neck rolls before hobbling barefoot to the kitchen.

Not yet ready for the glare of overhead lights, I turn on a small, single-bulb lamp. The aroma of coffee fills the kitchen within minutes, and soon I cradle a mug and head to the back porch. Shrouded by pre-dawn shadows, I sink into a cushy chair and wait for the sun to peek through the native oak trees behind my cottage.

Now that I am a widow, I sit alone in the serenity of a world not yet fully awake. It is a bittersweet reminder that grief intertwines with joy on this life journey. I sip my favorite coffee blend and let my mind wander through random things on my to-do list and names on my mental prayer list.

I take a series of deep breaths and slowly exhale while listening to the sounds of the newborn day.

Before my coffee cup is empty, I begin to do some ankle rolls and knee flexes to loosen my joints. I point my toes and pull them up, feeling the tightened muscles ease with every repetition. By the time the sun is fully up, my legs and feet are more flexible than before, and I am ready for a morning walk.

Recently I heard retired United Methodist Bishop Lawson Bryan give a one-word summary of the ministry of Jesus: *stretch*. Bishop Bryan reminded us of familiar Bible stories in which Jesus encourages all who could hear to stretch their understanding of who God is and what it means to be faithful.

Jesus has dinner with dishonest tax collectors and sinners. *Stretch*. He touches lepers whom religious leaders label unclean. *Stretch*. In the bright midday sun, he asks for water from a Samaritan woman whom others shun. *Stretch*. Repeatedly Jesus challenges the religious practices and cultural norms of the day. He awakens the hearers to fresh insight about who God is and how to respond to God's bountiful love and grace.

Bishop Bryan's one-word message is a powerful reminder to me that spiritual growth requires daily stretching of my heart and mind. Think about elite Olympic athletes on television doing stretching exercises moments before they step onto the world stage to compete. Even at the peak of their athletic careers, they physically stretch to increase both blood flow and oxygen throughout their bodies. Similarly, stretching our faith muscles revives our flexibility, strengthens our relationship with God, and gives us renewed energy.

When we become complacent about the importance of stretching, our thoughts and beliefs are prone to becoming rigid like muscles and joints after a night of inactivity. Our vision of who God is becomes too small. Our openness to God's miracles in ordinary life shrinks. Our faith becomes dry and stale. Soon we barely notice God's activity in the busyness of our days.

Where I Found God Today is a unique opportunity to purposely flex our spiritual muscles and expand our ability to see God at work in our midst. The personal narratives shared by fellow sojourners from many different places and backgrounds challenge us to embrace a heightened awareness of God's presence in daily routine. Some of the narratives will prompt a smile, while others might bring tears to our eyes. Each devotion will challenge us to look around and pay closer attention to God as we move through everyday life.

There are stories of finding God in unexpected places—a barn, the dairy aisle, a well-loved chair. There are inspiring stories of holy moments experienced watching paragliders, confronting a smelly bag of compost, or driving on a crowded freeway. Some narratives bring us face-to-face with death, divorce, and grief. Others stir warm, nostalgic feelings and point us to God in the pages of a dog-eared cookbook or in a mysterious box of miniature furniture. There are tales about the majestic beauty found in nature and gritty accounts of fractured relationships and broken hearts. Like a new box of crayons, the writings in *Where I Found God Today* display a colorful array of emotions and complexities of the human condition. Each devotion uniquely inspires us to cultivate our sensitivity to God's presence in the details of life.

My early morning routine reminds me that stretching, both physically and spiritually, is key to growing toward spiritual maturity. Taking a cue from those Olympic athletes, I recognize that stretching will promote my well-being and reduce the risk of injury in the future. Stretching spiritually prepares me for the race ahead, keeping me pliable and teachable. As I train my eyes to seek God's presence in the everyday moments, I gain resilience and reason to trust God with the unknowns of the future.

Tomorrow morning when I wake up, I will once again be stiff from hours of inactivity. I will do the repetitions of knee flexes and ankle rolls to make my body more limber. I will also listen for God's still, quiet voice speaking words of encouragement or challenge into the dawn. Inspired by those who dared to share their stories, I will be attentive to God's presence. At the end of the day, I will ask an important question: where did I find God today?

CHAPTER 1

finding God in little gifts

Wearing a Piece of a Platinum Watch

Desperate, I throw myself on you: you are my God! Hour by hour I place my days in your hand.
—PSALM 31:14–15 (MSG)

It was my father's final flea market at the annual Labor Day celebration in Hillsville, Virginia. Cancer was claiming his beloved pastime of selling antique timepieces. As I helped him pack up, the sign he'd hand-lettered on a piece of shirt cardboard gave me pause: Buying Time. How many times had I heard him tell a customer with a wink: "A man can own a Timex or a Rolex. But right here's the only place they can buy time."

Not really, I thought cynically. *Bone and lung metastases are taking care of that.*

Daddy took a piece of a platinum ladies' wristwatch from his scrap pile and placed it in my palm. Tiny diamonds dazzled from the clock's face, a gorgeous leftover from times past. But not functional without its band. "I want you to wear this on a chain, honey," Daddy told me. There was a gentle urgency to his voice, his message crystal clear. "To remind you to trust the clock you cannot see."

I felt my face scrunch up in a question.

"Your times are in *His* hands, Roberta," he added softly.

Nice try. But *my* life was a mess of endless tumors that had plagued me since birth, of treatments that failed to stop them, and chronic pain as a result. I couldn't see God at work in any of it. I'd heard versions of Psalm 31:14–15 all my life, usually from a preacher explaining the providence of God. I didn't warm to the concept.

My father's gift left me equally confused. I loved him dearly, but I wasn't crazy about everything that had happened where he was concerned, either. He was a hard, hard worker, kind and generous, a person of integrity. But for much of my life, he'd battled a problem with alcohol. It had embarrassed me. Frustrated me. Stolen much from our family that could never be recovered.

With the loss of structure in retirement, Daddy's drinking had escalated. He called me once in crisis, pleading for help, threatening to take his own life. Entered a treatment center after a harsh exchange of words. I was supposed to trust *that* kind of clock?

It wasn't long after that day at the flea market when we buried Daddy. The same day, I buried that piece of a wristwatch in a dusty jewelry box and didn't think about it again for a long time.

Years later, I retired from nursing at the same age as when Daddy left the railroad. The tumors I'd battled all my life escalated out of control. Doctors increased my pain medication until I was receiving the highest dose of OxyContin of any patient in Huntington, West Virginia, a town that could easily compete for the title of opioid capital of America.

At 63, I found myself in the throes of withdrawal, much like my father 35 years before. I was sure I'd never make it to the other side. Sprawled on the tile floor of a friend's bathroom, my clothes soaked with the excrement of a body, mind, and spirit gone awry, I heard my father's voice, as clear and urgent as when he'd pressed that treasure of time into my palm. *You're strong, honey. God is with you. He'll never leave. Your life is changing this very moment. Just like mine did.*

Webster has no words for the ways God has restored my broken life. Seven years have passed since my father's influence reached me from the great beyond. I'm still connecting the dots, but the divine timing, the impeccable order of it all—of my entire life—is beyond human comprehension. I wear Daddy's gift as a pendant around my neck, an earthly echo of the clock I cannot see. Every time I touch it, I am reminded that my times have always been in God's hands.

—*Roberta Messner*

WHAT WILL YOU FIND?

Do you have a memento that's symbolic of a loved one's influence? Why not craft it into a piece of jewelry to wear and remember? Let your family's legacy of faith inspire a future generation. Be sure to pass on the story along with the keepsake.

Searching for Wild Horses

Every good gift and every perfect gift is from above, coming down from the Father of lights, with whom there is no variation or shadow due to change.
—JAMES 1:17 (ESV)

After many years of birthdays together, my husband, Kevin, knows I like to celebrate with an outdoor adventure. But even he was surprised when I said that this year I wanted to search for wild horses. In our three decades of hiking in Arizona, we had only seen a herd of horses one time, and then at a distance. Even that brief encounter had stirred up a sense of wonder at viewing these majestic creatures in the wilderness. When an online group spotted some wild horses in nearby Cool Bluff, I decided I wanted to repeat that thrill.

At the site, we discovered hoof prints in the soft mud next to the Salt River. We skirted around piles of manure on the shore. But no wild horses. After two hours of searching, we returned to the car, discouraged.

"Consolation prize," Kevin said as he pulled out a birthday cupcake.

Touched by his gesture, I thanked him with a kiss. But in my heart, I was still disappointed. I whispered a prayer as I blew out the candle. "God, could you send me a gift of wild horses?"

I didn't really expect an answer. God had bigger things to worry about. Yet, as we drove out of the parking lot, we spotted them: two mares and a young foal! The chestnut youngster balanced on wobbly legs in the shade of a mesquite tree. We stood at a distance, snapping photos like Hollywood paparazzi while the foal nursed from its dappled gray mother. Talk about amazing!

My heart overflowed with gratitude to my God. With his birthday gift of wild horses, He delivered not just ordinary kindness but extravagant love.

—*Lynne Hartke*

WHAT WILL YOU FIND?

Spend time in prayer asking God for a unique way you can bless a friend or family member who has a birthday coming up. A personal card? A small present? The gift of your time? Be willing to be the answer to someone else's birthday wish or prayer. And as you bring the person their gift, let God's love for them shine through you.

Holding an Autographed Baseball

Let, I pray, Your merciful kindness be for my comfort, according to Your word to Your servant.
—PSALM 119:76 (NKJV)

"Please sit down," the doctor said. I sat, numb with shock, as he explained I would never have more children. Unable to fully process what I'd heard, I moved on instinct, leaving the office and driving to my seven-year-old son's school. I signed him out for the day.

"Mom, you're the best!" Morgan said. "What's the reason?"

"I thought we might play hooky," I fumbled, still reeling. "The Dodgers are in town."

I drove downtown in a daze and bought cheap seats. We'd made many good family memories at baseball games. The ballpark seemed like the best place to be.

Just as we entered, a Diamondbacks staffer intercepted us, asking if Morgan could be "security kid" for the game. My son trotted to his "post" in the Dodgers' dugout and I was upgraded to a field-level seat nearby.

"Thank You, God, for Your kindness," I whispered, closing my eyes. "I needed it today."

I opened my eyes to see Dodgers manager Joe Torre and my son swapping stories about baseball injuries and playing hooky! Torre gave him a handful of gum and an autographed baseball. Morgan ran to my seat, the tread of his Buzz Lightyear shoes leaving miniature impressions on the dirt track.

"This is the best day of my life, Mom," he announced, shoving his haul into my hands. "I gotta go guard the dugout now, OK?"

Fifteen years passed before I told my adult son why I pulled him out of school that day. He disappeared into his childhood room and rummaged around, finally emerging with that autographed baseball.

"It's yours now, Mom," he said. "I hope it reminds you that God is with us on our terrible days."

The ink is fading, but the memory of God's kindness never will.

—*Laurie Davies*

WHAT WILL YOU FIND?

Is there an object in your home that reminds you of God's kindness? Maybe a difficult time in your life that He helped you through in unexpected ways? Even if you have to rummage through a few drawers or dig deep into a closet, find it and keep it close today. As the psalmist prayed, His kindness and love are for our comfort.

In a Jar of Salsa

Now to him who is able to do immeasurably more than all we ask or imagine, according to his power that is at work within us...
—EPHESIANS 3:20 (NIV)

The school year I taught in Africa, homesickness hit me something fierce. Botswana's dry deserts, where goats darted across dusty roads and baobab trees with bare, twisted limbs stretched to the sky, were so different from the sandy beaches and leafy forests of my native Virginia. I stayed strong, refusing to break down and cry like a baby. Until...

I lived with two young American women who also wrestled with the missing-my-comfort-zone blues. A man from my friend's church was flying over to visit, and he offered to bring us things we missed from home. I asked for salsa. Botswana's restaurants were limited, and my Mexican-food-loving tastebuds demanded a spicy fix.

The visitor arrived with a big, green suitcase full of home-sent goodness. We made unpacking a game by keeping the lid closed, reaching in blindly, and pulling articles out one by one. When my turn arrived, I slid my hand under the flap, discovered something covered in a plastic bag, and pulled. Then I had to put some muscle into it, because this item was heavy! When I finally got it out, I was holding an industrial-sized container of salsa.

I burst into tears.

I'd expected a small, grocery-store-sized jar that I'd have to ration until the last bit was gone. This was enough to last for many suppertime fiestas. I felt God next to me in that moment, saying with a nod and a wink, *I know how much you miss your tacos. I gave your shopper an extra nudge.*

It wasn't the first time the heavenly Father had done this for me—exceeded my requests and super-sized the answer because He loves me. He's done it again and again since then. The salsa moments often come in the middle of difficult seasons, and that's what makes them meaningful. He always finds a way to let me know He's there.

—*Shannon Sue Dunlap*

WHAT WILL YOU FIND?

Among the stress and clamor of life, it's easy to forget the "salsa moments" where the Father has blessed us abundantly. Can you remember a time when God sent an extra-large answer to your prayer? If there's an item you can hold, or a place you can go that reminds you of it, take a moment to connect with that memory. Thank Him again—and be on the lookout for a new suitcase to arrive with more heavenly surprises.

In a Shoebox

And my God will meet all your needs according to the riches of his glory in Christ Jesus.
—PHILIPPIANS 4:19 (NIV)

"What should I wear to work today?" I stood in front of my closet. Inside hung a selection of mismatched items, most of which had been given to me by friends or purchased at the thrift shop. I appreciated the clothes, but there were several items I couldn't wear because they didn't go with anything else.

"I could wear this if I had some decent black shoes," I muttered as I looked at one outfit. "What I need are some good, comfortable black shoes, dressy but not too high-heeled. Too bad we're so broke."

I managed to pull something together and headed off to work. That afternoon, my boss, Irene, asked what size shoes I wear.

"Nine."

Her feet were three sizes smaller than mine, so I figured my answer would end the conversation.

"I've got a pair of shoes for you in the car," she said.

"Really? My size? Are they black?"

"Yes."

It couldn't be. "Do they have a heel but not too much of a heel?"

"Yup."

"I prayed for those shoes," I told her. *Well, sort of.* It hadn't really been a prayer—I hadn't been talking to God, hadn't been asking for His help. I certainly hadn't expected a response. But He heard me, and He answered anyhow.

Since Irene commuted 60 miles to work, she had already been on her way with those shoes in her car as I stood at my closet grumbling that morning. I was utterly humbled that God had orchestrated this on the same day I'd voiced my desires—and not even as a respectful request. What grace. What generosity. What a sense of humor!

I felt awed by the knowledge that the God who created the universe cared enough about me to show His power and character through a simple pair of shoes. And now every time I wear them, I remember.

—*Terrie Todd*

WHAT WILL YOU FIND?

If there's something you wish for—even something as simple as a pair of shoes—turn your desire into an honest and humble prayer. God may not respond in the way you expect, but He may grant your request most delightfully, revealing His beautiful nature and His outrageous love for you.

On the Side of I-44

For by him all things were created, in heaven and on earth, visible and invisible, whether thrones or dominions or rulers or authorities—all things were created through him and for him.
—COLOSSIANS 1:16 (ESV)

After 5 years of fighting for my marriage, this was the night that I was sure God would bring us back together. But He hadn't. My husband drove us home as I stared out into the darkness from the passenger seat, swiping at my tears. As the car sped down a rural stretch of I-44 in Missouri, the scenery on the other side of my window seemed to mirror my future—dark, wild, and unpredictable.

For miles, I searched the grassy shoulder for signs of life, knowing it wasn't uncommon for our headlights to reflect off the eyes of creatures wandering the woods. *Send me a deer*, I prayed, as their presence had become sweet love letters from the Father in recent months. Recently I'd found a fawn on wobbly legs in my backyard, and last week I'd seen a doe wandering alone in a field—reminders that God hears me.

That's when I saw him.

This was no tentative fawn or delicate doe. No. He was a noble buck standing tall and proud on the paved edge of the interstate, and he was there just for me.

His stately antlers stretched wide from his frame, proclaiming his authority for all to see. There was no fear in his eyes, nor did his presence bring fear to mine—only assurance. Gracefully, majestically, he turned his head toward us as we drove closer. That's where I found God.

Fresh tears streamed down my face as time seemed to slow and I stared into the eyes of this precious gift—a formidable king sent to set my heart at ease. No matter what happened between me and my husband, I could face the future confidently, knowing that I am the chosen daughter of the Most High God.

—Heather Tabers

WHAT WILL YOU FIND?

Have you ever asked God to send you a sign of His love? Is there an animal that is special to you, whose appearance would reveal God's presence? Ask God to show Himself in nature today and then go out, expectantly, to find His gift for you.

In a Spider's Web

There are four things which are little on the earth, but they are exceedingly wise ... The spider skillfully grasps with its hands, and it is in kings' palaces.
—PROVERBS 30:24, 28 (NKJV)

Farm life wasn't turning out to be as much fun as I'd expected. Since the first time I sang "Old McDonald" all the way through as a two-year-old, I'd vowed that one day I'd have a little farm of my own. Shortly before my fortieth birthday, that dream came true. My husband and I bought an old farmhouse on 15 acres of land. A fenced pasture and an ancient but sturdy red barn were part of the deal, too. So we loaded our three young children into our battered pickup truck and moved to the country.

And, yeah, it was fun. But it was also hard. Really, really hard. My muscles ached long before daily chores were over. My mind ached, too. There was so much to do. So much to learn. Fences and gates. Water pumps. Farriers and large-animal veterinarians. When to plant tomatoes and when to cut hay and how to keep predators out of the henhouse.

Most days, I felt overwhelmed. I wondered if we'd made a terrible mistake.

But then, one golden summer morning, I discovered the peace of the hayloft. I'd spent an hour mucking out horse stalls, scrubbing feed buckets, and filling water troughs. All that was left to do was climb the steep steps to the loft and drop a flake of hay through the gap in the floor into each of the stalls below.

Strangely, I felt reluctant to leave the loft once that chore was complete. Sunlight streamed in through the wide-open windows at each end, the rays catching the dust motes and making them dance. Mourning doves cooed from the rafters. The smell of fresh alfalfa hay, stacked high in square bales, filled my nostrils. I dragged a few of those bales over near the back window and built myself an armchair. From it, I could look out over the pasture. June bugs buzzed in the blackberry thicket. Goats grazed in the kudzu. A 5-foot-long rat snake lay stretched out near a fencepost, guarding the premises from rodents.

Burlap, the barn cat, wove between my feet and meowed softly as I lifted her onto my lap. I closed my eyes while I stroked her soft gray fur and whispered a little prayer. *Thank you, Lord, for life all around me on this farm.* When I opened my eyes, I noticed a spiderweb high in the corner of the window. How had I missed it earlier?

It was huge. It was complex. It was swaying softly in the breeze. This was like the webs the title character in *Charlotte's Web* wove in hopes of saving a dear little pig's life. And then, for the first time, it dawned on me that this barn was almost exactly like the one in the beloved novel I'd read over and over as a child. I stood, moved closer to the window, and looked up. There, front and center, was the spider.

"Salutations!" I said, echoing the Charlotte's greeting.

And I knew in that moment that God was inside the barn with me. He was with Burlap and the horses. He was in the pasture with the goats and the snake and even the June bugs.

Most of all, He was with this wonderful spider, whom I—of course—immediately named Charlotte. God had created all of them. Every day, He helped me to learn about and love and take care of them. Suddenly, I didn't feel tired. I just felt grateful.

I stared at Charlotte for a long time. Unmoving, she stared right back at me. She didn't wave any of her eight legs. She didn't weave any words from the novel—not SOME PIG or TERRIFIC or RADIANT or HUMBLE or anything else—into her web.

But as I closed my eyes in prayer one more time before descending the hayloft's steep steps, I'm sure I heard a soft, sweet whisper: "Salutations!"

—*Jennie Ivey*

WHAT WILL YOU FIND?

You don't have to live on a farm to be surrounded by animals. Dogs and cats. Birds in the sky. Squirrels in trees. Goldfish in fountains. Gaze in wonder at the marvelous creatures God designed. And pay special attention to one of the most amazing creatures of all: the lowly spider. Listen for the ways that God speaks through all of them.

Shopping in Walmart

*For the eyes of the L*ORD *range throughout the earth to strengthen those whose hearts are fully committed to him.*
—2 CHRONICLES 16:9 (NIV)

While rushing to get things we needed for my kids' end-of-school-year activities, I noticed two ladies making a beeline toward me in Walmart. My heart sank. I just knew they were going to ask me for money or some other favor.

It was a pattern in life in recent days. I'd been late to my own kids' awards night because I was babysitting for a friend who didn't pick up her kids on time. Then strangers asked me to pay for gas for their truck. I could help them out, right? I didn't feel right saying no to people in need, but they secretly pumped extra gas in cans when I wasn't looking. They took advantage of me. And now these Walmart ladies were going to ask for money?

I silently told God I didn't know if I could handle many more people asking for something of me! But I couldn't end my prayer with a complaint. I also asked for patience and for His help to be more loving.

The women came close enough to speak. "It's my fiftieth birthday," one told me with a smile. "My friend and I are spending the day together giving people $50 bills to celebrate. Will you accept one?"

A wave of awe came over me. My tension disappeared. I was completely touched by their generous act, and by God's sweet reminder that He sees me. He'd seen me when I was kept late. He'd seen me at the gas station. And He had His eyes on me right there in Walmart.

—*Jenny Snow*

WHAT WILL YOU FIND?

The next time you pass a Walmart, a gas station, or maybe another place where an act of kindness seemed to go unappreciated, use it as a reminder that God sees it all. He knows everything that has happened to you, and He cares. Watch for the moments when He reassures you of that truth, and thank Him.

In a Prayed-For Home

*The L*ORD *is my shepherd; I shall not want. He makes me to lie down in green pastures. He leads me beside the still waters. He restores my soul.*
—PSALM 23:1-3 (NKJV)

"Dear Lord," I prayed, "Please lead and guide Lauren and Chris to the home that is right and best for them."

Due to her husband's new job, our oldest daughter and her family were moving to Colorado. Although excited to return to the state where she and her husband were born and raised, they were sad to leave their home in Oregon, a cozy, private little house in the woods they had worked hard to make their own. The plains of Colorado burgeoned with sandwiched-in new builds, quite nice, but not at all secluded or serene, two qualities Lauren and her husband were searching for.

After weeks of unsuccessful looking, Lauren told us they thought they had found their perfect place—a log home on over two tree-studded acres with full mountain views, along with outbuildings to house not only their cars, but their home gym, workshop, yard equipment, and more. It even boasted an enclosed chicken coop equipped with one old, eggless hen! After some breath-holding negotiations, it was all theirs.

Several months later, on a sunshine-filled blue-sky day, I sat in their yard by a tree swing that hung from a huge cottonwood. The Rocky Mountains formed the backdrop to the field in which our three young granddaughters laughed and ran, their miniature Aussie chasing behind. Chris was happily cutting branches from an overgrown bush. Lauren was collecting eggs from a flock of chickens that had grown to fifteen. Even BokBok, the aged hen, had started laying again!

As I sat there, I felt embraced by the warmth of the sun, and the Son. I knew He was there with us, smiling at our delight. I felt wrapped in His presence and His love. The word *idyllic* continually rose to the surface of my mind, along with *thank You, Lord*. My prayer had been answered.

—*Kim Taylor Henry*

WHAT WILL YOU FIND?

Is there a change upcoming in your life or the life of someone you love? Find a place that represents that change to you—for example, a place in your home or an office. If you're thinking about taking on a new volunteer role, it might be the place where you would volunteer. Take a moment to imagine what you want and what you hope for. Then turn those hopes over to God.

At a Christian Bookstore

*Why, my soul, are you downcast? Why so disturbed
within me? Put your hope in God,
for I will yet praise him, my Savior and my God.*
—PSALM 42:11 (NIV)

My husband had left me, and I was praying for reconciliation. I didn't want to be a single mom of three, and in spite of everything, I still loved the man I'd married.

The two of us agreed he would come home at a certain time to be with the kids, and I would leave during that time. On this particular night, he showed up half an hour early. I'd made enchiladas, and the kids and I were about to sit down to eat, but he demanded I leave immediately.

I fled from my own home, hungry, heartbroken, and feeling hated. I had nowhere to go and, as a stay-at-home mom, no money to even buy dinner because he'd taken my name off the bank account and we were still figuring out the financial arrangements of our separation. I had been praying throughout the separation for reconciliation, but tonight it felt like even God had abandoned me. Everything just kept getting worse.

Desperate for hope, I called an uncle who had gone through something similar in his first marriage. He gave the best advice anyone could possibly offer: "You need to praise. Don't even pray for your husband. The rest of us have him covered. You praise God for who God is."

I headed to the Christian bookstore that had become my sanctuary through this storm. Putting on headphones, I listened to praise music. And despite my fears, self-doubt, and unanswered prayers, I was filled with peace. God met me in that store, reminding me that He is good even when our circumstances are not, and that His power would carry me to a better place. While so much of what happened during our separation depended on the actions of someone else, I learned that night that hope depends only on God. Even though my husband and I ended up getting a divorce, I was not abandoned. God will never leave me.

—*Angela Ruth Strong*

WHAT WILL YOU FIND?

Do you have a "praise place," one where you can go to set aside your worries and focus on God? If not, think about where you might seek one out. Is there a bookstore or library where you can find inspiration, or a particularly beautiful and quiet place where you can stop and listen for Him? Go there, and let Him fill you with perfect peace in the midst of life's imperfections.

Riding a Carousel

> *[Jesus] said to them, "Let the little children come to me, and do not hinder them, for the kingdom of God belongs to such as these. Truly I tell you, anyone who will not receive the kingdom of God like a little child will never enter it." And he took the children in his arms, placed his hands on them and blessed them.*
> —MARK 10:14-16 (NIV)

When my town received the generous donation of a 1909 carousel mechanism, the project to create the "finest carousel in the world" ratcheted up. Volunteers designed, carved, and painted for years until the merry-go-round came to life.

The moment I enter the building where the carousel is housed, I sense the enchantment of possibilities. Animals of every kind circle the carousel. Igknighter the land dragon chases Harriet, a giant frog, never quite catching her. Zulu, the African serval cat, races alongside Quigga, the quagga zebra. Each creature is a marvelous mix of reality and whimsy, a flash of bright colors reflected in the mirrors on the central column for those watching. The scent of popcorn fills the air, and I purchase a bag as I decide which animal I will ride. Sound, sight, smell, touch, and taste—every sense is delighted.

But there's something more going on, just beneath the surface. It's God, filling every inch of this space with His joy,

His creativity, His hope for the future. I see Him here, amid the laughter and the warm smiles. In the steadfast perseverance of the volunteers as they carve and paint more improbable animals for this endless loop of wonder. And like all the other children of all ages, I grab for the ring and a glimpse of heaven.

—*Heidi Gaul*

WHAT WILL YOU FIND?

Is there an old-fashioned carousel near you? If not, pick a place that speaks to you of the joy of play and set aside time to visit. Allow the child in you to shine as you take part in some favorite activity from your own younger years. Watch as God makes an appearance in the joyful faces of others around you.

CHAPTER 2

finding God in guiding signs

At the End of the Tunnel

You can show others the goodness of God, for he called you out of the darkness into his wonderful light.
—1 PETER 2:9 (NLT)

I hit the snooze button, then rolled over on the sofa. Nine minutes passed quickly. My hand pounded the top of my 1980s clock radio until it found the snooze button again. If I didn't get up soon, I'd be late for my $6.25-per-hour newspaper job. I just wasn't ready to face the internal, infernal game of twenty questions.

Will I need a third job?

Will I make it in this world?

What purpose am I serving—working two jobs just to collapse and do it all over again?

I was in my early twenties and already so tired. I had moved to Phoenix armed only with ambition and a single suitcase packed with clothes. Now here I was, sleeping on my sister's sofa and barely able to pay for insurance on the car I relied on to get to work. The day before, I ordered water when I joined my newsroom colleagues for lunch. My friend C.J. nudged her "leftover" taco toward me and I put my sunglasses on—the big ones that covered my tears—and hungrily accepted.

Isn't there more to life?

Should I just admit failure and move back home?

I dressed for work. The upside of crashing at my sister's apartment was free rent. The downside was she lived nearly an hour from my newsroom. You'd think the commute would help me clear my head, but it only reminded me that the knocking and grinding sounds in my 1986 Nissan Pulsar needed attention.

I grabbed my briefcase, ran out the door, and mindlessly drove down the I-17 freeway in Phoenix. Soon, I'd change freeways and reach my favorite part of the drive—a 3,000-foot stretch of I-10 that runs underneath downtown Phoenix. Locals call it the Deck Park Tunnel. I don't know why I loved that part of the drive so much. Maybe it was because for a 30-second span every morning, the metropolitan whoosh of speeding cars drowned out the knocking and grinding of my own insecurities.

This morning was different. As I approached the tunnel, I noticed—maybe for the first time—the skyscrapers, urban neighborhoods, and cars all around me. All filled with people. A lot of them probably as tired as me.

"God, if you're real, I think your heart must really beat for all these people who are down here trying to make their way," I said out loud.

And just like that, everything went dark. My eyes fought to adjust to the dim, yellow-toned lights that snaked across the ceiling of the tunnel. I sensed, with an unnameable certainty, that God was inviting me to think about more than just me and my needs. He was telling me that life was going to be real dark if I continued to live without Him. And as I drove toward the literal light at the end of the tunnel, I understood God was inviting me into the light of His love.

The intense desert sun is always a little blinding upon reentry from the tunnel into daylight. But that morning it was different. The light was enticing, not blinding. The mountain peak on my left glimmered in the morning sunrise. I made a mental note to return there and climb it after work.

I clocked in at work, where an internal mix of adrenaline, nervous energy, and anticipation distracted me from my daily newsroom clerking tasks. I sensed things shifting. Hope was breaking down the doubts that the journalist-skeptic in me had about God.

I clocked out, climbed that mountain that had glimmered in the morning sunrise, and gave my life to Christ.

Today, even if the I-10 is loaded with traffic, I go out of my way to drive through the Deck Park Tunnel. It's much more than a freeway connector that gets me where I'm going. It's the connector between my life before I knew God and 30 years since. It's the place where God firmly pulled my attention away from myself and toward Him on an otherwise routine Tuesday—a physical landmark of the life-changing moment God invited me out of darkness and into His glorious light.

—*Laurie Davies*

WHAT WILL YOU FIND?

Have you ever had a time when God asked for your full attention? It may even be the day you first stepped out in faith. Where were you? Visit that place, or someplace similar, and let yourself travel back in memory to that moment. Thank God for drawing you out of the darkness and into the light of His love.

Between the Blue Mountain Shadows

Where there is no counsel, the people fall; but in the multitude of counselors there is safety.
—PROVERBS 11:14 (NKJV)

The day was perfect for hiking, sunny, with a welcome crispness in the air. The trail contained a smorgasbord of cactus: barrel, prickly pear, cholla, and the iconic saguaro. But it was Weaver's Needle—a thousand-foot spire that rose out of the desert floor like a skyscraper—that grabbed my attention.

As we hiked, we talked about a proposed change at the church where my husband, Kevin, serves as the associate pastor. The decision to include tables in the sanctuary for seating was not popular with the older generation. On the other hand, the younger attenders embraced the change as a way to facilitate conversation and community. The simmering tension affected everyone.

"Look at that view," I announced as we rounded the final switchback. Weaver's Needle loomed in front of us, impossible to miss.

"But look behind you," Kevin exclaimed.

I turned around. Layers of distant mountains framed the desert in stunning blue shadows. Cobalt. Navy. Sapphire.

I had been so focused on the Needle, I had neglected to keep an eye on the beauty behind me. The realization shifted something inside me regarding our church situation. We needed to listen to the concerns—and the wisdom—of our seniors *and* the younger generation before we moved forward with a decision. Despite the tensions, discussions about the seating had already produced constructive ideas to make the experience more inclusive. If we kept talking, more would come.

God used the blue mountain shadows to remind me of the wisdom I could gain when observing the view from all directions.

—Lynne Hartke

WHAT WILL YOU FIND?

The next time you are faced with a different viewpoint, practice listening intently rather than focusing on how you are going to respond. Make eye contact. If you don't understand, ask questions in a kind way. What is the wisdom that God wants you to hear in this situation? What is the middle way He might want you to walk?

Hearing an Elk Bugle

*Whether you turn to the right or to the left,
your ears will hear a voice behind you, saying,
"This is the way; walk in it."*
—ISAIAH 30:21 (NIV)

Some sounds on this planet stick with you, perhaps even becoming part of you. For me, one of those is an elk bugling in autumn.

Each fall, my family and I make many trips up to the Rocky Mountains to hear the eerie, ethereal call of the bull elk. Their unique call has marked many memories while camping, hiking, and exploring wilderness areas. But on this particular September day, as we drove at dusk around Rocky Mountain National Park listening for the elk, I was distracted. That week, I'd received news that my grandmother's health was failing, and she was expected to pass away soon. I struggled in my spirit with whether to fly and see her. Of course I wanted to, but the logistics around traveling were complicated. The decision hung heavy in my mind, shrouded with tension.

What should I do, God? I prayed silently. *Should I go?*

At that moment, an elk bugled, loud and clear.

Hearing that sound, surrounded by Rocky Mountain summits aglow in the sunset, I knew I had my answer. The same God who'd carved these mountains and canyons, the One who gave the elk its voice, and the One who'd wonderfully made my grandmother was the same One who would work out every detail for me to go and say my goodbyes.

A couple of days later, I walked up to my grandmother's bedside. In a rare moment of clarity, she grasped my hand with all her strength, peered with foggy eyes into my own, and spoke my name with a smile.

When I need clarity, I know I need to go out in nature. God will push past doubts and hesitancy and plant an answer in my spirit, guiding me to where I need to be.

—*Eryn Lynum*

WHAT WILL YOU FIND?

Are you struggling with a question or decision? Go on a walk. Think about something in the world around you that has a special significance—an animal, a plant, an object, a sound. Ask God to reveal Himself through His spirit and creation. Tune your attention to the world around you and see what He says.

On a Boat at Night

In him was life, and the life was the light of all people. The light shines in the darkness, and the darkness did not overtake it.
—JOHN 1:4-5 (NRSVUE)

Night fell as my commercial fishing boat, *Surprise*, left the harbor and began its run for San Miguel Island 98 miles away.

Nighttime nautical navigation is not a problem if you have a decent marine radar. The *Surprise*, however, had a well-earned reputation for living up to her name. Somewhere about the 80-mile mark, our radar gave up the ghost. To add insult to injury, the seas had gotten pretty rough. I could make out the glow of white water topping the big rollers in our running lights.

Cuyler Harbor, our target destination, was a pinprick on the chart, and still a long way away. I held my compass bearing and prayed we wouldn't be moved too far off course by the wind and waves.

Then, cresting a big swell, I saw something—the tiniest flicker. Far away but dead ahead. Another vessel already tucked into the anchorage for the night. At least I hoped. I let out a long breath and steered for that tiny glow.

As we got closer, I navigated by ear, waves crashing rocks as we inched through the harbor mouth toward another boat with—sure enough—that glorious little light shining bright atop his mast.

I felt God with me during that entire trip, saw Him in that tiny light in the distance. Ever since, the memory has stuck with me, a lesson I've never forgotten: No matter how dark and rough life's sea, there is a light ahead—Jesus guiding and beckoning. What a comfort to know that one day I will sail into His presence. I'll drop anchor in that safest of harbors. All this world's suffering and stress will be forgotten.

I will rest as a new sun rises on a glorious and eternal day.

—*Buck Storm*

WHAT WILL YOU FIND?

Go outside in the dark at night. Try to find somewhere far from artificial lights, where there are no obvious signs to guide you. How does it feel? Have you ever felt that way—disoriented, even scared, by the forces trying to pull you off track? Look inside yourself, to the light of God's love within you, and breathe. Trust the light that never wavers, and the One who has the power to calm the seas.

At a Writing Retreat

*Let it be written for a future generation that
a people not yet created may praise the LORD.*
—PSALM 102:18 (NIV)

I had a big, scary idea for something I wanted to write. It was so scary that I needed God's direction before choosing to pursue it. I'd discussed it with my literary agent, but I just happened to be attending a writing retreat that weekend, so I asked my writing group to join me in prayer.

On the last day of the retreat, I was in the shower when I got a nudge from God: He had an answer for me in Scripture. I got out of the shower and headed directly for my Bible. Randomly flipping it open, my eyes locked onto the opening words of Psalm 102:18: "Let it be written."

I shut my Bible, pushed it away, and started shaking.

That didn't just happen. It couldn't have. Because if God was answering my prayer so directly, I didn't have a choice. I'd have to pursue the big, scary idea—ready or not.

I didn't want to tell anyone, but I did. The big, scary idea is now a published book. And I no longer doubt that I've been called to write.

I'm constantly amazed at how God can use the written word to speak directly to our hearts, and awed that I get to join Him in the creative process.

A friend was recently so touched by one of my books, she planned to have a phrase from it tattooed on her arm.

I decided to join her. I now have "Psalm 102:18" on the wrist of my writing hand.

I still get scared by the size of my dreams, but I know I'm not doing it for myself—and I'm definitely not doing it alone.

—*Angela Ruth Strong*

WHAT WILL YOU FIND?

Do you have a big, scary dream? Pray to God about it. Invite others to join you. Really listen for His answer, and be open to His guidance, no matter how strange the instructions might be. Then expect God to answer, because He has a purpose for your life.

In a Smiling Shadow

"Go with the strength you have.... I am sending you!"
—JUDGES 6:14 (NLT)

Walking my usual path in my neighborhood one morning, I stared at the sidewalk as if it could give me answers. I had a tough decision to make. Making a certain choice—the one I was pretty sure was the right one—risked repercussions. I begged God for courage.

My walking route took me past a neighbor's house and their ornamental fence decoration of a sun with a smiling face. No sooner had I uttered my prayer than I saw it: sunlight shone through the ornament and cast the image of a smiling sun on the sidewalk right in front of me. I practically stepped on God's reassurance! It felt like a smile from God, letting me know everything would be all right.

I remembered the story of Gideon from the Old Testament. The Lord found him threshing wheat in a winepress. Gideon was basically hiding in a pit to do a job that should have been done in the open air, where wind could blow chaff away. He was not on strong footing. But the Lord sent him to battle, saying, "Go with the strength you have" (Judges 6:14, NLT).

For confirmation, Gideon ended up asking God for several signs, and the Lord answered each time.

I need reassurance sometimes, too. Looking back on my anxious walk that morning, I knew which way I should go, but I was afraid to take the next step. And God responded with a clear sign.

Even though the smiling sun decor still hangs on my neighbor's fence, I have never seen the shadow from it again. God created the perfect conditions—a cloudless sky, the season, the angle of the sun, and the time of day—to give me courage to move forward.

And, looking back, the decision I made was undeniably the right one.

—*Laurie Davies*

WHAT WILL YOU FIND?

Are there times when you question the path you should take? Going to a specific location and seeking God's answer is one way to find out, but if circumstances don't permit leaving the house, try asking God to use everyday objects: Let Him lead you to a specific room, close your eyes, and then ask Him to show you what you need to see.

Caring for Clara's Plant

For God so loved the world that he gave his one and only Son, that whoever believes in him shall not perish but have eternal life.
—JOHN 3:16 (NIV)

I have never been one of those people with a green thumb whose plants thrive, stretching their leafy limbs toward the sun. Instead, plants appear to tremble in fear when I walk through Walmart's nursery section. "Don't pick me," they seem to mumble under their breath, reminding me of myself in algebra class.

However, I was encouraged to take a plant home after the funeral of my mother-in-law, Clara. "I'm sorry," I whispered to it, apologizing for whatever lay ahead.

I placed it in front of the living room's picture window. Every morning, while praying and drinking coffee, the plant reminded me of my precious mother-in-law. She had been my second mom for 43 years. During the last few years of her life, she looked forward to eternal life in heaven. Her faith never wavered. But did mine? After her passing I wondered, sometimes, if she was really safe in heaven.

I tried to keep up with the care of the plant. I really did. Every morning I would see the plant and think I should water it, but usually by the time I left the room I'd forgotten about it. Then, about a month after Clara passed, I noticed something strange. The plant, against all odds, was still alive. Had it been a fake plant all along and I'd never noticed? I checked and confirmed it was, in fact, real.

Sixteen months passed. My husband, Don, would occasionally look at the thriving plant and then shake his head in bewilderment.

"How are you keeping that plant alive?" he finally asked.

"I'm using God's Miracle-Gro," I replied.

There's no way the plant should have lived, but it did. Every time I walk by it, I see God's hand at work, His ongoing assurance to me that Clara is blooming eternally in heaven. What a great way to start the morning.

—*Kristy Dewberry*

WHAT WILL YOU FIND?

Do you keep houseplants? Is it something that comes naturally for you, or do you have a "black thumb" when it comes to keeping them alive? If you don't already have a plant, consider buying one to remind you of God's love. Every time you come back to tend to it, imagine yourself growing and thriving in the life He gave you.

Playing in the Snow

> *He breathes on winter—suddenly it's spring!*
> —PSALM 147:18 (MSG)

A storm had been raging since dawn, burying my neighborhood beneath more than a foot of snow. Suddenly, the sun broke through the clouds, transforming each snowflake into iridescent glitter. As I surveyed the frosty confetti, sparkling on every rooftop and tree branch, I felt God's nudge: *Come out and play!*

I tried ignoring God's tug toward adventure. My plan for the day was to curl up and read. Why choose cold, wet, and uncomfortable when I felt so warm, settled, and cozy right here? But I knew this moment wouldn't last. I donned my snow gear and ventured outside. The deep snow made me as wobbly as a toddler first learning to walk. I giggled at my clumsiness, while praising my divine instigator for His magical creation.

I only spent a few moments in the bitter cold admiring the sparkling landscape and crunching through pristine drifts. My feet were chilly, but my heart was buoyed with joy. Back inside, I took off my wet gear and climbed back beneath the blanket on the couch. But I continued to play—with words. I wrote a poem about my snowy playdate, something I hadn't done in several decades. From childhood until I began writing professionally in my late twenties, I'd crafted lots of poems, songs, and short stories. But somewhere along the way, I traded carefree wordplay for pay. Writing became more of a chore than a delight.

Later, I realized God wasn't just inviting me to interact with Him and His creation that day, but to reconnect with the poet and storyteller in me. I'm so thankful my God is also a wise Father, consistently trying new ways to inspire me to draw closer to Him and to who He created me to be.

—*Vicki Kuyper*

WHAT WILL YOU FIND?

The next time the weather is inclement, dress appropriately, then head outside. What can you discern about God's character from what He's created? Respond to God's gift of Creation by creating a thank-you gift for Him. Write a psalm. Paint a picture. Play an instrument. Dance. Sing. Smile! How does it feel to be a gift for God?

In a Room Full of Mothers

Trust in the Lord with all your heart; do not depend on your own understanding. Seek his will in all you do, and he will show you which path to take.
—PROVERBS 3:5-6 (NLT)

Standing at the podium, I looked down at my notes, taking a second to compose myself. *Am I really going to share this part of my story?* I had been invited to speak to a group of seventy-five moms to share my story and offer encouragement. Now that I was standing there, about to talk about one of my most regrettable parenting moments, I was having second thoughts.

I glanced around the room and was met with expectant faces. I had already told them about my family and voiced how hard motherhood can feel sometimes. The story I was about to tell was vulnerable, but something in me knew this was the story God wanted me to tell.

Taking a deep breath, I told them about one day in my kitchen when I screamed at my kids. I knew I was out of line, but still, I screamed. And this wasn't just a story about losing my temper once. This was a story about my long-term struggle with anger and how it had affected my family. This particular day was the day I finally recognized it was a problem and I wanted to change. Still, I felt embarrassed to show others that part of me. Would they think I was a terrible mom?

As I shared, I watched the women's faces. They weren't judging me. Instead, they were nodding, even wiping tears as they listened. My story connected with their own. I didn't offer pat answers or solutions. Instead, I offered vulnerability and connection, an opportunity for moms to feel less alone in their own struggles. I finished the story, encouraging them in their motherhood journeys. But as I walked off the stage, I felt encouraged, held up, and met by the tender response that reminded me that I wasn't alone.

When I stepped out in obedience to share my story, I didn't know I would find God in that moment. But at the point I felt most vulnerable, God used the tender connection with the other moms to heal my heart and remind me of His grace. I found God in that room full of mothers, when He showed me how He supports me as I take a step of faith to honor Him.

—*Rebecca Hastings*

WHAT WILL YOU FIND?

Is God asking you to step out in faith and do something in obedience? Take a few minutes and ask Him if there is something He wants you to do. If you receive an answer, write it down. Next to that, write down when you will do it, and make a commitment to meet that promise.

Underneath the Paragliders

> *Depend on the LORD; trust him, and*
> *he will take care of you.*
> —PSALM 37:5 (NCV)

When my sister, Lisa, and her husband, Dan, came to visit us in Arizona, my daughter, Katelyn, and I decided to take them on one of our favorite hikes: the 2.4-mile Treasure Loop in the Superstition Mountains.

"Are you up for an evening hike?" I asked, checking my phone for particulars. "Looks like only 6 minutes separates the sunset at 6:01 and the moonrise at 6:07. We could get some great photos."

"Isn't it a full moon tonight?" Lisa asked.

I nodded.

"Even better. Let's do it!"

As we gathered water bottles, headlamps, and backpacks for an evening adventure, I couldn't help but wish all decisions could be made so easily.

For months I had been tied up in knots about a work decision. I felt God nudging me to stop focusing on a book idea and to focus my attention on speaking instead. I was making myself crazy with the what-if questions.

What if I put down the book idea and I never pick it up again? What if I'm not cut out to be a speaker? What if this idea turns out to be a dead end?

And the biggest question of all: *What if I am not really hearing from God?*

I had filled pages in my journal, making lists of pros and cons. I found myself paralyzed with indecision, waiting for certainty and perfect clarity while I sat in the not-knowing.

All I had was a nudge. I wanted a 5-year plan.

Once on the trail, we snapped dozens of photos of the sunset as it transformed the desert skies into a kaleidoscope of shifting colors. Yellows. Oranges. Purples. Reds. Jupiter and Venus appeared in the western heavens while Orion hugged the top of the mountain peaks in front of us. Those same peaks blocked the rising full moon.

"We'll need to go around that bend if we want to see the moon," Katelyn advised. We dug out our headlamps and climbed in elevation while a curved-bill thrasher entertained us with cascading notes from a nearby wash.

Suddenly, we heard an unfamiliar sound, like giant wings unfurling, but louder than any eagle or vulture I had ever heard. What was happening?

"Paragliders," Dan exclaimed, seeing them first. One paraglider leapt from the cliffs, the canopy of an enormous parachute billowing in the evening breeze. Two more followed, one after the other. They rode the winds above us silently as we watched, jaws dropped.

How long had the paragliders sat on the cliff edge, not willing to jump until they had the right conditions? How did they know the wind would carry them? Did they worry about landing on a cactus? Had they waited for the sunset colors to give them a perfect, photographic moment? Had they been held back by indecision, not knowing if the time was right?

How long will I wait on the edge of indecision?

I was asking myself, but I knew the question had been prompted by Jesus, the One who directs my steps in life.

The paragliders gave me the answer I was seeking. As I watched their silhouettes against a violet sky, I knew Jesus was telling me it was time to take the risk and launch myself into the unknown. I could trust His care, even in the places where I had no control, no detailed list or 5-year plan.

I didn't have all the steps in place, but I had the promise of His presence. Like the paragliders, it was time to take the first step. It was time to soar.

—Lynne Hartke

WHAT WILL YOU FIND?

Is some concern consuming all your attention? Write down all your thoughts, worries, and concerns on a piece of paper. Fold the paper up like a paper airplane. Say a prayer as you launch it across the room, while you release all your concerns and unknown details into God's care. Feel Him carry you like the wind carries a glider, and focus on the beauty above.

CHAPTER 3

finding God in times of need

Swimming in Shark-Infested Waters

If I take the wings of the morning and dwell in the uttermost parts of the sea, even there your hand shall lead me, and your right hand shall hold me.
—PSALM 139:9–10 (ESV)

Look who suddenly remembered how to pray...

I always enjoyed Shark Week on the Discovery Channel. Working in the dive industry, I found the technical aspect of the episodes fascinating. One show in particular caught my attention. It featured the first successful fish-eye footage of a great white shark attacking from beneath, rocketing up from the depths to decimate its prey. Such massive jaws. Such power. And such apprehension in my gut when I realized I was scheduled to do a deep, open-water recovery dive the next day—very close to where the attack had been filmed.

We all make poor decisions from time to time. Vanilla when we wanted chocolate, socks that don't match, stripes with plaid. But let me tell you, watching that particular show before that particular dive does not rank as one of my brighter moments.

The sun shone bright on the Santa Barbara Channel the next morning. The sea was calm and flat. A beautiful day, by all appearances. Everyone was in high spirits. Everyone but me, that is. All I saw was dark, shark-riddled water. After last night's show, I felt like the whole ocean had teeth. I did my best not to show my trepidation as I suited up. *C'mon, Buck, it's just another dive.*

The job itself wasn't complicated—attach a recovery line to an expensive anchor that had been lost on the bottom the week before. The one fly in the ointment was that the anchor rested exactly 205 feet beneath our hull. Now, if you were to walk 205 feet on dry land it wouldn't seem very far, not even the length of a football field. But underwater, particularly on scuba, this is an extremely deep and technical dive. The worst part—at least if you were idiot enough to watch Shark Week the night before—were the decompression stops on the way back up. A decompression stop is the period a diver must spend at a relatively shallow constant depth during ascent after a dive; skipping it risks decompression sickness. Most of the time a decompression stop is boring, just hanging and waiting. Today was a very different mental game.

The recovery went fine. Only 5 minutes on the bottom. Shark Week faded as I focused on the task at hand. But then came the final decompression stop.

Have you ever wondered what it would feel like to be a worm on a hook? Well, brothers and sisters, I can tell you exactly. I hung there, sunlight slanting through the water, staring down into the black, with last night's attack scene playing through my mind on a fast-forward loop. I'll tell you what, if you ever need strong motivation to rededicate your life to Jesus about ten times in a row, go hang on a line in an area infamous for white sharks.

"God, help me..."

Hmm, look who's back?

"I know, I know, I've been a little distant."

Yes, but I haven't. And now we're talking.

"Isn't there an easier way to get my attention? A car crash or something?"

I could almost hear Him laugh.

I watched the seconds tick down, the minutes feeling like hours. A lifetime later, my time was up. Skin still crawling, but taking my first hopeful breath since I'd hit the water, I followed my bubbles toward the surface.

Back on deck, missing no limbs or chunks of my body, I peeled out of my suit. My heart slowed. I felt the sun on my shoulders.

I breathed deep. I felt alive. "Thank You."

Don't be a stranger.

You know what? I wasn't.

I love the fact God exists outside of me. I don't imagine Him, I don't control Him. I can't box Him. I also love how He will go to any length to snap me back to attention. He wants to be with us. Always. And we should want Him just as much.

—*Buck Storm*

WHAT WILL YOU FIND?

Diving in shark-infested waters is not for everyone. But have you ever caught yourself letting your prayer life lapse for a little too long, only to turn to God in a frightening or stressful moment? If you're in a safe place and have everything you need in life, take a moment to thank Him.

In My Backyard

I will exalt you, my God the King; I will praise your name for ever and ever. Every day I will praise you and extol your name for ever and ever.... The LORD is near to all who call on him, to all who call on him in truth. He fulfills the desires of those who fear him; he hears their cry and saves them.
—PSALM 145:1-2, 18-19 (NIV)

My teenage heart was troubled over many things late one evening when everyone else was asleep. I longed to draw closer to God. I wanted to call on Him as it says in Psalm 145. But not in my room.

I wanted to talk to God out in His creation—like David in the Bible often did when tending his sheep. Like I had as a little girl, just swinging on my swing in the backyard and singing songs to God. Now, as a teenager, deeper issues weighed on my heart. Greater consequences followed my decisions. And yet, He was still the same loving, mighty God.

I padded down the hall, slid the back door open, and plunged into the dark of my backyard. My dog kept watch nearby as I gazed past the shadowed treetops to the starlit sky above and poured out my heart to the Lord. I softly and sincerely sang psalms of worship and praise. I thanked the Lord for all He had done for me and all I was grateful for, and I asked God to help me with problems I needed His wisdom for.

But most of all, I just sang to Him about how much I loved Him and wanted to be closer to Him. Like the psalmist, I called on Him. Little by little the anxious knot inside me loosened and lifted, replaced by the comforting sense of God's presence and love. How amazing to know He was near me. I found God in my backyard that night, and my heart found peace.

—*Jenny Snow*

WHAT WILL YOU FIND?

Go outside in early morning or late at night—or even right now—and sing a worship song to the Lord. It could be a psalm, an old hymn, or a new song you've made up. Know that when you call on the Lord in truth, He is near to you.

Putting Out a Help Wanted Sign

Two are better than one... If either of them falls down, one can help the other up.
—ECCLESIASTES 4:9-10 (NIV)

In 1997 I purchased a historical West Virginia log cabin. Hysterical might be a more accurate description. That is, if you weren't the one who'd made the investment. The floors were so tilted, I dubbed it The Leaning Log. One thing was clear: I'd need to do a lot of leaning—on God and anyone else I could recruit—to make it livable.

A friend painted a scene from *The Little Red Hen* on the kitchen door, where a flour-dusted hen, frustrated with doing it all, asked, "Who will help me?" That same question was going through my mind as I took a crowbar to drywall to reveal the century-old chestnut logs. Refinished heart pine floors. Outfitted the kitchen with freestanding cupboards in lieu of the cabinetry normal people bought at Lowe's.

One day a man came to work on the electrical system. He shook his head at the paint cans lining the mantel, the cloud of drywall dust, lightbulbs hanging by threads of ancient wire. "You and Zoloft must've bought this place," he quipped.

I'd never felt so alone. When a neighbor gave me a tin Help Wanted sign that had once hung in his grandparents' general store, I propped it in a window, a silent admission that I'd gotten in over my head.

Then the oddest thing happened. When folks saw that sign with its brick-red lettering, they actually stopped and asked what they could do.

These days, my cabin is both livable (well, almost) and lovable. I'm not in the market for workers, but I still adore that Help Wanted sign. No longer in a window, it's proudly perched on a shelf. A reminder that when I'm vulnerable enough to admit that I need help, God is there, nudging all the helpers I need in my direction.

—*Roberta Messner*

WHAT WILL YOU FIND?

What does your spirit need today? A friend? A listening ear? The advice of a wise, trusted professional? Maybe you don't have a Help Wanted sign—but is there an action you can take to let people know what you need? Talk to God about it until you're ready to risk reaching out, the first step toward change.

On a Hay Bale

God is our refuge and strength, an ever-present help in trouble. Therefore we will not fear, though the earth give way and the mountains fall into the heart of the sea, though its waters roar and foam and the mountains quake with their surging.
—PSALM 46:1–3 (NIV)

One summer, when I was a teenager, my family and I bicycled across the United States.

We were pedaling east, somewhere near the border of Washington and Idaho, when a storm kicked up. Within the span of a few minutes, the weather changed from warm and sunny to cold rain, then pelting hail.

From his position in the front, my dad gestured to an old barn at the end of a gravel drive. He hollered something, but the storm swallowed the sound of his voice. Lightning flashed and thunder boomed as we reached the barn and dragged our bicycles, heavy with packs, through the tall sliding door.

Chilled from the cold rain, legs achy from a long day of pedaling, I grabbed my sleeping bag and climbed onto a giant hay bale. The sound of hail drummed against the roof as I drifted to sleep.

I woke hours later to the shine of blue sky through the open barn door and the sound of my dad cooking spaghetti over our camp stove. Rested and happy, I reflected on the events of the day: sudden change, harsh circumstances, a weary body, and the refuge of a stormproof barn.

This is what God is like. He's not a partial-shelter kind of God. He's a come-to-Me-and-take-a-nap kind of God. He holds the door open, and He offers to be our refuge in the midst of every storm.

—*Kate Rietema*

WHAT WILL YOU FIND?

What do the storms in your life look like? Where do you look for refuge? As a prayer exercise, sketch a picture of your refuge in a storm. Does it look like a house? A barn? Or does it look more like a person? As you contemplate your personal shelter, ask God to show you how He's offering peace and rest in all areas of your life. Add notes and labels to your picture as you pray.

Staring into the Fog

*I lift up my eyes to the mountains—where does
my help come from? My help comes from the* LORD,
the Maker of heaven and earth.
—PSALM 121:1-2 (NIV)

When I enter my tiny studio atop a hill behind our home, multiple Blue Ridge mountain ranges welcome me most mornings. But not this morning.

A recent mammogram led to the dreaded call requesting further testing. My mind skipped the small stuff and headed straight to the worst-case scenario at record speed. With the afternoon follow-up appointment hovering overhead like a bad dream, I headed up to the studio for respite. The air was wet and weighted, but it wasn't until I reached my desk, framed by an 8-foot-long, single-paned window, that I noticed the mountains were gone, eclipsed by a thick curtain of fog.

I stared into nothingness, without even the view to distract me. In the silence, a question popped into my mind: *Who are you?*

Without hesitation, I said aloud, "I am a daughter of the King."

The words echoed through me, and I realized the message I'd been given in the midst of my own fog: If I'm the daughter of a King, I should act like one.

God gave me the idea to write down what I could see (fog), and then what I knew was behind the fog despite not seeing it (mountains). He lovingly lifted my thoughts far above the worry, revealing how my sole focus was on the seen—my circumstances—instead of God. He showed me how He, though unseen, is a tower of strength in our time of need, never growing faint or weary.

I lifted my eyes to the heavens, confident that whatever circumstances I face would dissipate in the presence of the Lord—my strength and my song.

—*Cathy Baker*

WHAT WILL YOU FIND?

When facing trials or doubts, write down what you see or the thoughts troubling you. Then, write down what you know to be true. What's in between is the gap where God meets you, guiding you through the unknowns into a place of safety.

In a Hard Meeting

> *I pray that he may grant you, according to the riches of his glory, to be strengthened with power in your inner being through his Spirit, and that Christ may dwell in your hearts through faith.*
> —EPHESIANS 3:16–17 (CSB)

I stood outside the oak-paneled door, wondering if I could do this. I had been in meetings like this before. Just like the other times, I had gathered all the paperwork and arrived early, ready to talk about the needs of a child. I knew what would happen, what we would talk about, and what questions needed answers. But every other time I'd been in this situation, I was on the opposite side of the table, wearing my teacher hat instead of the parent hat. This felt new and scary.

Instead of going into the meeting as the educational expert reporting how a child was doing in the classroom, I would enter as the parent expressing my concerns and asking for help. I knew I would sit alone, needing to advocate for my son.

As I waited, I said a silent prayer asking God to help me. The door opened, and I sat down. We exchanged introductions, and I took a deep breath. As I spoke up about my concerns, something unexpected happened. There was a divine presence with me, surrounding and supporting me. I realized that I wasn't the only one there for my son—God was there with me. He wanted the best for my son, too.

The meeting was still hard because it was so important to get my son the services he needed, but I no longer felt like I was facing it on my own. God's presence girded me, giving me confidence in the meeting as I advocated for my son. When I remembered that God promised to be with me, that He lives within me and comes into every hard place with me, I had all I needed. It was knowledge I would carry with me to the next meeting room, and the next, and the next, giving me the courage to act and speak in ways I couldn't have on my own.

—*Rebecca Hastings*

WHAT WILL YOU FIND?

The next time you go into a hard meeting or a place that intimidates you, remind yourself that God goes with you. Even as you drive there or walk into a room, whisper, "Thanks for coming with me, God." The more you do this, the easier it is to remember He is with you everywhere you go.

At a Security Checkpoint

You will keep him in perfect peace, whose mind is stayed on You, because he trusts in You.
—ISAIAH 26:3 (NKJV)

As I rounded the corner to the airport security checkpoint, my breath caught in my throat.

I glanced to the left, to the spot that was imprinted on my memory. Right there, 7 years ago, I'd suffered an attack of previously undiagnosed vertigo that led to heart palpitations, leaving me unable to board the plane home. Airport personnel called an ambulance, and I ended up in the emergency room in an unfamiliar city. My husband caught the last flight out from where we live—several states away—to rescue me and bring me home.

In the following months, we sought and finally discovered a diagnosis and treatment for what I was experiencing. Yet anxiety from that day has made flying a challenge ever since. Airports and flights rattle my sense of control and leave me feeling anything but secure. Being at *this* security checkpoint makes it even worse. But I do fly, and each time I get on a plane is a victory and testimony to God's steadying peace in my life.

Removing my shoes and placing them on the conveyor belt, I looked once again at the spot. I remembered the security officer boldly praying aloud over me as I was laid down on a stretcher and wheeled out.

On this day, nothing happened. I took a deep breath and prayed a prayer of thanks to God before walking forward toward my flight. *I did it.*

It was a victory, but it wasn't just mine. I had a profound sense of God with me, His deep peace infusing me, reminding me I was safe and secure in His hands—not just here, not just when I fly, but always.

—*Eryn Lynum*

WHAT WILL YOU FIND?

Visit a place that holds a difficult or challenging memory. Prayerfully prepare by laying that memory in God's hands. Ask Him to heal and help you in a way only He can. Bring a close friend for support. When the visit is over, thank God for the mending and growth He is bringing forth.

Holding Flashlight Batteries

For God gave us a spirit not of fear but of power and love and self-control.
—2 TIMOTHY 1:7 (ESV)

The radio's severe thunderstorm warning urged me to replace the flashlight batteries, a task I'd forgotten. Large trees sometimes drop limbs on electrical lines in our neighborhood and cause power outages. Rumbles of thunder convinced me to hurry.

Fretting about the upcoming storm, I postponed my prayer time. After quickly inserting new batteries, I gave a flashlight to my husband, Will. I snuggled into a comfortable chair with my own flashlight and opened a novel while he watched a movie.

As soon as I turned the first page, the lights flickered. Seconds later, a power outage stranded us in total darkness. We pressed the switches on our flashlights but remained in the dark. "I put new batteries in them, so why aren't they working?" I asked.

Using the light from his phone, Will discovered that in my haste, I'd inserted the batteries the wrong way. There was no connection to produce light. He corrected the problem in his and soon a beam of light appeared in the darkness.

As I removed the batteries from my flashlight, God whispered a message into my heart. When I fail to spend time with Him in prayer and Bible reading as I'd done that day, I miss the connection with Him I enjoy. Fear had crept in and distracted me. I'd sought peace and wisdom from other sources.

Now, whenever I see a flashlight battery, it reminds me how important it is to connect with my heavenly Father each day. Without spending time with Him, I am powerless to think His thoughts and obey His Word.

—*Jeannie Waters*

WHAT WILL YOU FIND?

Place a flashlight beside your favorite chair or in another spot where you spend a lot of time. Let the flashlight remind you how its batteries produce power—like daily time in prayer and Bible study keep you connected to God. List the verses He uses to shine light into your life and give you the power to live for Him.

On a Hospital Lawn

They went up on the roof and lowered [the sick man] on his mat through the tiles into the middle of the crowd, right in front of Jesus.
—LUKE 5:19 (NIV)

As someone who'd always measured my worth by how much I can do, a breast cancer diagnosis had me feeling worthless. The chemotherapy stole my hair and my ability to keep up with my old schedule. The hoodie I wore to warm my bald head made me resemble the Emperor from Star Wars. I was hospitalized at one point for neutropenic fever. And my brain fog through the whole experience kept me from being able to focus on anything—including prayer.

That's when others picked me up and carried me to Jesus. I couldn't have made it on my own.

During my weekly visits to the oncology department, I found much more hope than expected. Strangers crocheted me hats and quilted me blankets. Acquaintances performed Christmas carols on their musical instruments. Friends played card games, and my kids brought Legos.

Then Covid hit, and on the very last day of chemo treatments, nobody was allowed to attend my bell-ringing—a huge milestone in cancer treatment that signals the end of a rough period of chemotherapy. Thankfully, the nurses still made it a celebration. They played the song "I'm Still Standing," and one even rocked out with an air guitar.

After that, I walked outside to find the lawn filled with a socially distanced, mask-wearing crowd, holding signs expressing support for me. I'm still not even sure who all came, but I'll never forget them.

Through my battle with cancer, God not only brought healing to my physical body, but He healed me from the compulsion to prove my worth. In a time when I'd never had less to give, I also never felt more loved.

—*Angela Ruth Strong*

WHAT WILL YOU FIND?

Do you know someone who needs to be carried to Jesus for healing, either literally or spiritually? Where is the place you might find them, and how can you carry them?

Have you ever been in a place where you needed to be carried for healing? What was the place? Who met you there?

At the Corner with Walgreens and Family Dollar

"But when you give to the needy, do not let your left hand know what your right hand is doing, so that your giving may be in secret."
—MATTHEW 6:3-4 (NIV)

A lot has happened at the corner on Route 60 in Barboursville, West Virginia, where there's a Walgreens and a Family Dollar. Kids selling Girl Scout cookies. Lemonade stands. And on the hottest August morning ever, my alternator failed there, trapping me in my silver Altima.

A man who appeared to be unhoused regularly stood at that corner, selling paper posies from a bicycle basket. Folks stopped to buy them. One local noticed more. When the man rode his bicycle around town, he was rolling on rims. "How 'bout a new bicycle?" the local asked.

The posey maker was thrilled at the gesture. He went straight for a top-of-the-line model with a big, shiny silver basket. When he rode around town, he was positively beaming at everyone in sight.

Rumors swelled. The posey maker had plenty of resources, they said. How else could he afford that expensive bicycle? He must have a nice check coming in. Anyone could see that the local had been duped. I'm sorry to say that I believed it myself.

I knew the local well. No purer heart in these parts. Folks chided him about this latest gesture. One day I asked, "How does that make you feel? You work so hard for your money..."

The local's answer changed the way I view giving. When my mind is tempted to wonder about a recipient or an outcome, in my mind's eye I go back to that conversation, the way it made me feel God's love right there in front of me.

The local rubbed his chin at my question, gazing into the distance at something I couldn't see. Finally, he answered: "It wasn't so much about giving him a bicycle. It was about letting him know that someone *wanted* to give him a bicycle."

—*Roberta Messner*

WHAT WILL YOU FIND?

Take a drive or a stroll around your own town. When a place pulls your heartstrings, ponder what life has taught you there. How is it part of the story of your life? Has it brought you friendship? Joy? An unforgettable conversation or happening? Did it change you? Or is it challenging you to change?

In a Hospital Room at Night

And the God of all grace, who called you to his eternal glory in Christ, after you have suffered a little while, will himself restore you and make you strong, firm and steadfast.
—1 PETER 5:10 (NIV)

Sitting in the sterile room felt too familiar. It was only 3 weeks ago that we were here, happily celebrating our new baby boy. The delivery had gone perfectly; he was born on time and weighed in at a healthy 8 pounds, 10 ounces. Family came to meet him, admiring him and counting his little fingers and toes, and his new big sister held him. It was all so happy. I never imagined I would be bringing my newborn son back to the hospital so soon.

After a couple of weeks at home, he got sick. We had numerous calls and doctor visits, and finally were sent to the children's hospital for some tests. The doctor assured me they were just precautions and everything would be fine. I never expected to go directly from those tests to having my infant son prepped for emergency surgery.

Things happened quickly, and the years have left the details blurry around the edges; my memories are like snapshots in an old slideshow. The feeling when I had to hand him to the nurse, watching them walk away with my boy, and finally, after what felt like days, the relief when the doctor came and told me everything went well. The pent-up tears came quickly, a release of worry and fear.

Late that night, after my family left, I was alone with my son. As I sat next to his little crib in the almost-dark hospital room, I watched him breathe. I listened to the monitors. I felt so drained. My postpartum emotions and fatigue only intensified everything that was hard about the situation. I wanted to be grateful that the surgery was a success. I tried to pray. But I didn't have anything left to give. There was nothing I could do to help my tiny son other than be there with him.

The second hand ticked in the quiet room, time crawling and sleep eluding me. I wanted to be done with the whole situation. I wanted to know he was OK, take him home, and put this terrifying day behind me. But I couldn't make time go any faster. I simply had to sit in this hard place and wait until it was over.

The waiting felt terrifying and lonely. I worried about whether he was breathing and if he was in pain. I wondered if he would heal properly and how long we would be there. I wondered if I was doing enough. Fear and worry kept creeping in, but there was nothing I could do except wait.

It was in that place that I found God. In the middle of the night, in a sterile hospital room next to my infant son after emergency surgery, God entered in with me. He didn't wait for me to pray or get myself together. He simply brought His presence to be with me in the hard place. It didn't change the circumstances, but it shifted something deep inside. My worry was replaced with peace, with the sure knowledge that God was there, right there with us, and we were not alone. Sitting in that hospital room, God drew me closer to Him, and that sense of His nearness has stayed with me every day since.

—*Rebecca Hastings*

WHAT WILL YOU FIND?

As you lay in bed tonight, think about something hard you are facing that leaves you feeling alone. Instead of asking God to fix it, ask Him to come and meet you in that place. Welcome His presence in the darkness.

CHAPTER 4

finding God in connections across time

In My Daddy's Rowboat

*For I, the L*ORD *your God, hold your right hand; it is I who say to you, "Fear not, I am the one who helps you."*
—ISAIAH 41:13 (ESV)

The weathered rowboat sitting on the shore of the grassy lake reminded me of long-ago fly-fishing dates with Daddy. He'd hold my hand as I stepped into the unstable boat and settled onto my seat in the bow. Then he'd board and push us off into the lake.

Cattails encircling the lake created a private haven just for Daddy and me. Dragonflies with their transparent wings hovered over the surface. Occasionally, a bass or bream jumped out of the water.

We'd sing "Row, Row, Row Your Boat" softly so as not to scare away the fish. Daddy paddled the boat forward to glide across the lake, creating ripples as we chatted and laughed. Sometimes when he'd lift the oar to change sides, I'd giggle as water droplets landed on my nose or in my hair. Nothing interfered with our fun or made me fearful—not even the rocking boat, the pesky mosquitoes, or the sky darkening with the setting sun.

I felt safe in the rowboat because Daddy was with me.

As the cicada and frog singers raised their voices and the sun sank low into the pine trees, Daddy would say, "Time to go. God is closing the curtain on today." He'd paddle to shore and lodge the front of the boat onto the muddy bank.

He'd hold my hand to guide me to solid ground. The rowboat would rock and tip as we moved, but I wasn't afraid. My dad held my hand.

Decades later, seeing Daddy's weathered rowboat beside the lake, my thoughts turned back to the comfort and safety I knew when he held my hand. As I smiled at the cherished memory, God reminded me He's the one who holds my hand now and keeps me safe—even in the storms of life.

The disciples learned the same lesson when a storm blew in over the Sea of Galilee. Water covered the boat as it pitched up and down in the angry waves, rocking far more than our little rowboat did on the lake (Matthew 8:23–27).

While the disciples fretted, Jesus slept. "Save us, Lord; we are perishing," they cried (verse 25, ESV). When Jesus spoke, the sea calmed, and the disciples knew they were safe in His presence. They'd been safe all along because He was with them.

Life's storms often threaten to disturb our peace, capsize our faith, and tempt us to fret and even fear the unknown. Illness. The death of a loved one. Discouraging news. Broken relationships. A lost job or financial reversal. Whether we experience life interruptions, or our circumstances stay the same, our Savior extends His hand to us and calms the storms of our heart. With tender mercy and compassion, He steadies us and keeps us safe. He protects us with His loving care and guides us to the next step with His strength and wisdom.

The sight of Daddy's rowboat led me to stop and thank my heavenly Father that I'm safe in the boat with Him—on the shore or in a stormy sea, He holds my hand.

—*Jeannie Waters*

WHAT WILL YOU FIND?

Is there a place where you felt safe as a child—protected and guarded in spite of any frightening things that might happen? If it's practical to do so, go visit that place, or similar place nearby that reminds you of it. Once you're there, focus on the words of Isaiah 41:13: "Fear not, I am the one who helps you." Remember that in peaceful water and in stormy seas, your heavenly Father holds your hand.

In a Redwood Tree Circle

"For there is hope for a tree, if it be cut down, that it will sprout again, and that its shoots will not cease."
—JOB 14:7 (ESV)

Thirty-two family members traveled from all corners of the United States to northern California for my nephew Matt's wedding to Zella. After my parents died, weddings had become the connection point for our extended family. As we gathered that day, I felt the weight of being the oldest generation, the carrier of the family legacy and traditions left by Mom and Dad. Could our family ties continue without our parents holding us together?

After the formal church ceremony, we drove to the outdoor reception, located under a canopy of coastal redwoods. During the dancing, great food, and speeches, my eyes kept returning to the towering giants—especially to a ring of younger redwoods. This new generation of trees had grown in a ring around the massive stump of a fallen redwood.

"Let's get the bride and groom's photo under the trees," someone suggested.

Without prompting, Matt and Zella stepped into the redwood circle. As Matt kissed his new bride and smiled for the cameras, I suddenly sensed God's message—His reassurance in the face of my fears. The parent tree was gone, but the new trees had grown around the space left behind. The next generation had the advantage of tapping into the existing root system rather than starting alone from a single seed.

The deep roots my parents left behind remained. We were still a family with traditions and stories. God was still with us. The circle of redwood trees was the perfect place to welcome a new bride into our growing family circle.

—*Lynne Hartke*

WHAT WILL YOU FIND?

Find an old tree and stand underneath its canopy. Run your hand over the aged bark. Is there a young sapling nearby? One perhaps grown from the seeds of this older tree? Listen to the wind rustling the leaves. Imagine the many years those branches have seen, the many generations that have already grown from the seeds it produced in its long lifetime. Quiet your breathing. What is God saying to you underneath His trees?

Sitting at the Roots Table

But thou art holy, O thou that inhabitest the praises of Israel.
—PSALM 22:3 (KJV)

My connection to God and the world, my creativity, had sunk into a dry spell. I'd been a writer for decades. Now I couldn't form a sentence.

Then, in a series of serendipities, the one-drawer pine table where Alex Haley wrote *Roots* became mine. I positioned the table in front of a window facing a stand of whispering pines. The drawer filled with mementos of Haley's life whispered louder. A black-and-white glossy of him receiving the Pulitzer. Snapshots of him at book signings. Pens long out of ink. A box of personalized stationery. I ran my fingers over the raised letters, amazed that a man of such literary stature would have chosen such a simple message.

Find the good and praise it.

I needed to be productive again. But if Haley thought it important...

I pulled a piece of parchment from the box and found a pen that fit my fingers just so. *Dear Debbie,* I wrote. *These words are a long time in coming. I've never forgotten how you gave up your bedroom when I recuperated after surgery and took such good care of me. You are such an encourager.*

More letters followed. Old friends. Old neighbors. Folks doing the extraordinary they thought was just ordinary.

I wrote one to God, the Giver of all good, who promises to inhabit our praise.

And then He came to me and inhabited the praise I was sending to others, bringing His presence into my heart and His life to my pen. I began to write more prolifically than ever before, and soon I was back to my old writing routine.

But I never forgot that life-changing lesson: I'm never more alive, more connected to His world, than when I find the good and praise it. Thanks, Mr. Haley!

—*Roberta Messner*

WHAT WILL YOU FIND?

Who can *you* praise this very day? The bagger at your corner grocery store who's careful not to smash your bread? A friend or family member who had a victory at work or school? A mentor from long ago who may not realize the impact they had on your life. You don't have to write a formal note. A quick message, or even a touch of your hand and a few words, can lift a person up.

Wearing My Mother's Ring

*Remember the L*ORD *your God. He is the one who gives you power to be successful, in order to fulfill the covenant he confirmed to your ancestors with an oath.*
—DEUTERONOMY 8:18 (NLT)

"**I** need something borrowed," my youngest daughter said. We'd been planning her wedding day for months, a time of heart-swelling joy, suddenly made all the more so when she asked, "Mom . . . can I wear Grandma's ring?"

I looked down at the ring on my right hand, one that my mother had specially made. The gold that makes up the band is clumped in several places to look like gold nuggets—a choice my mother made to honor her father, who had loved to go gold panning. He would scoop up black dirt from the California hills near his home and pan for gold in a big water tank in his backyard. I remember being a child, standing by Grandpa and watching closely as he taught me how to swirl the pan, searching for specks of gold.

Set in the gold are three diamonds. Two of them are from engagement rings: the first from my maternal grandma's engagement ring, the second from my paternal grandmother's.

As the diamonds sparkle, I remember the lifetime of love my mother's parents shared, and how Grandad wrote monthly love letters to Grandmother for more than 50 years. I think about how Grandmother and Grandad scrimped and saved during the Depression and how proud Grandad must have been when he had finally set enough money aside to buy his wife a bigger diamond, the one he'd always wanted to be able to give her—now the third diamond in the gold ring on my finger.

My mother had loved her three-diamond ring for its memories from both sides of the family, but wore it only for special occasions, fearful that something could happen to an object she held so dear. I always admired it and loved what it stood for, never even thinking about the fact that it would someday be mine. Looking at the ring now, I remember the first time I wore it after her death, wishing with all my heart that my mother was still there and that I could see the ring on her hand, not mine.

I decided to wear the ring on a daily basis, because every day is special, and time goes so fast. Why not enjoy its beauty, its meaning, and its memories while I can? Every day I look at it and feel a connection to my mother, to the past, to the future, and to God, who is past, present, and eternal. It speaks to me of the cycle of life He created, the love of the family He placed me in, and His plan to pass that love from generation to generation.

My daughter walked down the aisle to take her vows and head into her future wearing the family ring that would one day be hers. As I watched, my heart filled with the joy of our family's blessings, and of God's gift of life and love stretching from hand to hand across time.

—*Kim Taylor Henry*

WHAT WILL YOU FIND?

Is there something you have inherited from a loved one that has special meaning? Or an item you own and would one day like to pass on to someone you care about? When you look at it, what memories and meaning does it evoke? How does God speak to you through it?

Talking to Mrs. Beasley

Love the LORD *your God with all your heart and with all your soul and with all your strength. These commandments that I give you today are to be on your hearts. Impress them on your children. Talk about them when you sit at home and when you walk along the road, when you lie down and when you get up.*
—DEUTERONOMY 6:5–7 (NIV)

My husband and I were browsing through an antique mall in Guthrie, Oklahoma, when I grabbed his arm. "That's Mrs. Beasley!"

Don glanced around the store, assuming I was referring to another shopper. I wasn't. Mrs. Beasley was a doll, a plush, blond-haired doll in a blue dress with yellow polka dots, based on a character from the TV show *Family Affair*.

She wasn't just any doll. She had been my best friend growing up. I'd never understood why other little girls were infatuated with fancy plastic dolls when they could have a huggable friend like Mrs. Beasley. Why would I want a doll that wets itself like Betsy Wetsy? Or talks all the time like Chatty Cathy? Barbie reminded me of my sister's stuck-up friend who made fun of my glasses. Mrs. Beasley, though, was the perfect doll for me.

I had been a worrier and a nailbiter from a very young age. I kept all my feelings bottled up. But Mrs. Beasley eased my fears and listened to my secrets. She loved me no matter what. I felt safe in her presence.

As I explained all that to Don in the store, I realized I was describing my relationship with God. My parents weren't churchgoers when I was little, and I'd felt something or someone was missing from my life. Mrs. Beasley helped fill that void until I started attending my friend's Sunday school class and learned about God.

Don insisted—with very little resistance on my part—that I buy the doll. She now sits on my bedroom shelf. I'm grateful that Mrs. Beasley was there for me when I needed a friend. And every time I see her, I feel God's presence surrounding me. I know that He will always there when I need Him, listening to my prayers, easing my fears, and loving me no matter what.

—*Kristy Dewberry*

WHAT WILL YOU FIND?

Do you have a treasured memory of love from your childhood—a special toy, or a gift from someone who meant a lot to you? Did you have a special item, like a doll or a stuffed animal, that you confessed your secrets to? If so, remember that item—pick it up and hold it if you still have it, or something that reminds you of it. Use it as a reminder to tell God a special secret in your prayer time.

Reading My Grandmother's Living Bible

Praise the Lord. Blessed are those who fear the Lord, who find great delight in his commands. Their children will be mighty in the land; the generation of the upright will be blessed.
—PSALM 112:1-2 (NIV)

There are only three times I remember seeing my grandmother sit down: at meals, watching the Lawrence Welk show, and meeting with the Lord. Ma-Ma's finely woven swivel chair, the color of dark brown sugar, sat next to a large window shaded by Southern pecan trees, just within reach of her Living Bible and devotional guide. Her unwavering faith was evident in both word and deed, but growing up, I assumed she read the Bible and prayed with the same swiftness as she approached everything.

So, during my teen years, when Ma-Ma shared that she prayed for me daily, I gave it little thought after my obligatory smile faded. In the years that followed, a string of unwise choices birthed from my unbelieving heart resulted in two divorces by the age of 27. With the pain, however, also came my salvation. Ma-Ma mourned my past choices but rejoiced in God's calling me to Him.

Years later, after her passing, I inherited what I wanted most, her Living Bible. The avocado-green faux-leather cover, now crackled and worn to bare edges, told its own story of faithfulness. As I opened her Bible for the first time, God held me with every turning page, highlighting Ma-Ma's marks from her daily reading and handwritten verses on salvation and prayer that framed His living and active words. Her Bible revealed a devotion to Him that was neither hurried nor taken for granted. God's nearness was palpable, opening my eyes to the power of a praying grandparent.

When I hold Ma-Ma's Living Bible, I also hold a part of my own story and that of generations to come—a story of God's faithfulness and a grandmother's prayers, holding us tight through all our trials.

—*Cathy Baker*

WHAT WILL YOU FIND?

What will the next generation find in *your* Bible margins, prayer journal, or letters that will spur them on in their faith? If you've made notes on your Bible reading, take some time to go back over them and reflect on what you felt and thought as you wrote them. Or, if you've never written down your thoughts, why not give it a try?

Singing "Great Is Thy Faithfulness"

*Because of the L*ORD*'s great love we are not consumed, for his compassions never fail. They are new every morning; great is your faithfulness.*
—LAMENTATIONS 3:22–23 (NIV)

My little-girl-self gazed around my grandparents' church, taking it in. Everything about this place felt so different. We stood in front of pews instead of chairs. The room was tiny compared to our home church, a building bigger than a basketball gym. The elderly were abundant, though I did spot a few kids my age. A lady walked to an instrument at the front of the room—an organ, my dad said—and the music and singing began.

I studied the faces of the people around me, so devoted in their worship as they sang "Great Is Thy Faithfulness." What made them sing about God's faithfulness with such feeling?

That childhood memory stuck with me. And that hymn became dear to me as I gained life experience and went through trials and hardships through the years. I experienced God's faithfulness, mercy, and provision during those trials.

Recently, I was going through another difficult season. Someone in my family faced health challenges, and we sought the Lord about which doctors and treatments would be best. I went to church as usual and was enjoying singing praise to God when the worship leader began a song I hadn't heard in person for a long time: "Great Is Thy Faithfulness."

My heart filled as memories transported me to that day when worshippers sang so fervently of God's great faithfulness in the pews of my grandparents' small-town church. He had been faithful to me every day since. And He would be faithful still. I knew in that moment that the music was a message from God, a reminder that I could give my worries to Him and let my family member rest in His care. What a good God we serve.

—*Jenny Snow*

WHAT WILL YOU FIND?

Play the hymn "Great Is Thy Faithfulness" on whatever device you use to listen to music. Pay attention to the lyrics and reflect on the ways God has been faithful to you over the years. Thank the Lord for what He has done. Consider swapping stories of God's provision with a family member or friend.

Holding a Black-and-White Photo

Start children off on the way they should go, and even when they are old they will not turn from it.
—PROVERBS 22:6 (NIV)

It is an old black-and-white photo, 2 inches by 3 inches, with a water stain in the lower left corner. The photo shows the home I grew up in, and our family assembled there on the front porch.

It's a time machine, that photograph. It whisks me back to a time when I felt safe and secure, and a place where family members loved God and loved one another. There on the front steps is my mother, for whom Sunday worship was as natural as breathing, and who every Saturday night would give me my nickel for the next day's Sunday School offering. There is my father, who would fold his gnarly, weathered hands at the supper table and lead the family in prayer. There is Grandma, who took it upon herself to do something my parents never would have thought to do, and would have disapproved of had they known about it: she paid me money to memorize Bible verses. The going rate was a penny a verse, a lot of money in those days, and a practice that gave new meaning to the phrase "the value of Scripture."

They were not perfect, those people, but each in their own way taught me that God is real, and that I was His beloved child. The old homestead is long gone, and the people who dwelt there have passed away, but God never passes away. And when I want to feel His presence anew I go to my desk, slide the photo out of its envelope, and smile at the thought of the reunion that awaits me someday in a home that can never be taken away.

—*Louis Lotz*

WHAT WILL YOU FIND?

Spend some time looking at old family photos. Thank God for those people, those places. When you find photos of yourself, consider who you were then, when the photo was taken, and who you have become, and how God has led you to where you are now.

In a Dog-Eared Cookbook

From everlasting to everlasting the LORD's love is with those who fear him, and his righteousness with their children's children.
—PSALM 103:17 (NIV)

Flipping through my grandmother's dog-eared cookbook, I land on her famous cinnamon-spiced baked-apple recipe. The floral pattern on the cover, once a vibrant red, is now worn and faded. The weight of the book in my hands is comforting and familiar. A large brown splotch in the corner marks the time I dribbled vanilla extract across the counter, a memory we both laughed about for years.

The page itself is a tapestry of splattered butter and my grandmother's loopy handwriting. My name is scrawled beside the recipe, childishly printed, with a note in her hand: "Extra cinnamon for Elly!" Each scribble feels like a hug, a tangible reminder of God's provision and the enduring love that passes through generations.

She made those baked apples for me countless times. Even now, I close my eyes and recall the comforting scent of cinnamon and warm apples wafting from her tiny kitchen. The apples, soft and yielding with a touch of tartness, were the perfect contrast to the sweet, gooey filling. We'd sit at the chipped Formica table, mugs of marshmallow-topped cocoa steaming in our hands, and savor each bite of the warm dessert.

Looking at her handwritten notes now, I can almost hear her gentle voice reminding me to slow down and enjoy the simple pleasures. It's in these moments of love and shared experience that my grandmother taught me the most about God—that His love, like hers, is overflowing, comforting, and always present, even in the imperfections of life. Though she has passed on, I can revisit her cookbook, relive those lessons, and feel her presence—and God's—all over again.

—*Elly Gilbert*

WHAT WILL YOU FIND?

Do you have a collection of recipes? Or a favorite dish that reminds you of a friend or family member's love? If you can, make the dish for yourself or for your own loved ones—and make notes on the recipe to pass along to anyone who asks.

In a Letter from a Sponsored Child

Give thanks in all circumstances; for this is God's will for you in Christ Jesus.
—1 THESSALONIANS 5:18 (NIV)

I turned the knob and watched sluggish brown water flow from my bathroom sink. *Not again.* Our community social media page confirmed that another water line had broken, repairs were underway, and a boil-water order was in place. I would love to tell you I handled this minor inconvenience with grace, but I did not. Instead, I stomped around complaining about what I perceived as gross inadequacies in our city's water department.

Still grumbling, I went through a stack of mail and finally smiled when I saw a letter from the teenage girl my family sponsors in South America. I unfolded the colorful paper and gazed upon a recent picture of her, astonished at how much she'd grown in just a year. As I read her words—translated by the ministry through which we sponsored her—conviction gripped my soul.

"Thank you for praying for my family," she began. "It has finally rained here, and I am excited because it means we can have water. It is my job to walk to the river, which is over a mile away, and bring water back for my family. Now that it has rained, we will have water again. Please pray that it continues to rain here."

Within the words written by a young girl in a language I cannot read, I found God.

He met me there, reminding me how blessed I am to live with so many amenities at my fingertips—even if occasionally the water runs brown. In love, He rebuked my despair over the developed-nation problems I was experiencing. With tenderness, He led my heart to repentance and gratitude, turning my bad day into one of praise. I boiled my water with a peaceful heart.

—*Heather Tabers*

WHAT WILL YOU FIND?

Maybe you need help putting life into perspective, too. Sponsoring a child is a wonderful way to bless others and stay mindful of the many blessings we often take for granted each day. Maybe you'll also find God in the scribbled words of a child you've never met but will always love.

Holding My Sister's Nativity

"My Father's house has many rooms; if that were not so, would I have told you that I am going there to prepare a place for you?"
—JOHN 14:2 (NIV)

The quiet in the sterile hospital room became noticeably quieter as my sister Peggy breathed her last breath. At that moment, I prayed that God knew her heart. I prayed that if she had not been a believer, as her husband Dick said, that Jesus would have come to her in her sleep, in her dreams, and called her soul home. I prayed that I would hear her voice again someday in heaven.

I returned home to life as usual—to throwing my son's birthday party, to getting up and going to work each day, to making dinner and cleaning up afterwards—but life felt anything but usual without her.

When my brother-in-law died only a month later, perhaps of a broken heart, my oldest sister, Suz, was named executor of their estate. She was tasked with sorting through all their possessions and deciding what to distribute in kind and what to sell. She called me one day to tell me she had some of Peggy's things she wanted to bring to me—a large china hutch, if I had room for it, and a few small items.

When Suz and her husband arrived, we first set to work getting the hutch unloaded and in place. Then she brought out the smaller things—a delicate teacup and saucer, a few old Johnny Cash vinyl albums, two books about Arches and Canyonlands national parks, and a rock of petrified sand. She saved the best for last—a 12-inch-high ceramic figurine of Joseph, Mary, and the baby Jesus. Carved into the bottom of the hand-painted figurine was Peggy's name.

Suz knew that I collect nativities; that's why she gave it to me. But she had no way of knowing why this little figurine would mean so much more to me than any of my other fifty-plus nativity sets.

I was pretty sure that Peggy wasn't an atheist, because only three weeks before she died we had talked on the phone about our parents being in a better place. But still, I wasn't certain until I held this simple representation of the birth of Jesus in my hands. As I gazed upon it, I heard God say to my heart, *You will see her again. She is with Me. Your prayer has been answered.*

The first Christmas after Peggy's death, I displayed my new favorite nativity right in the middle of the coffee table. When it came time to pack away the Christmas decorations, I couldn't bring myself to relegate it to the storage shed with the others. I found a perfect place in a curio cabinet instead. Whenever I noticed it, I would remember God's answer to my prayer. I would remember how much God cares about those who are important to me.

Ten years later, Peggy's figurine is still my favorite. I love to give tours of my collection to friends and family, and I always make sure to spend extra time on this one, telling and retelling the story of how God let me know He had heard the cry of my heart. He had prepared a place for Peggy just as He has for me and for all who believe in Him. Even though I now pack it away with the rest of my nativities when the Christmas season ends, I remember and believe I will see her again.

—*Linda L. Kruschke*

WHAT WILL YOU FIND?

Find a special item to remind you of how much God loves all His children—a figurine or some kind of memento. It could be an item that you've owned for years, perhaps one that belonged to another loved one, or it could be something new. As you hold it, remember loved ones who have passed, and feel the promise that you will see them again.

CHAPTER 5

finding God in messages of love

On an Answering Machine

Give me a sign of your goodness, that my enemies may see it and be put to shame, for you, LORD, have helped me and comforted me.
—PSALM 86:17 (NIV)

I looked at the answering machine on my bedroom dresser. I knew there weren't any new messages. Nowadays, callers rarely leave a voicemail on it. But I still felt inclined to hit the machine's "play" button.

The recording whirled back to the first message. It was from my mother, joyfully singing "Happy Birthday" to me. That saved message must have been nearly 10 years old. After the humorous serenade, Mom said, "It's your mother," as if I wouldn't know.

The voice was vibrant and full of life. It was the voice of a woman who cared deeply for her husband and three children, kept a tidy house, and enjoyed cooking for family and friends. Mom's voice has been a source of encouragement and comfort throughout my life. It was the voice that often told me, "Don't worry. It'll work out," "Things will be better in the morning," and "Trust the good Lord."

I thought about what life was like for my parents when Mom left that message. She and Dad were living semi-independently in the home they purchased together when I was just five years old. But they now needed additional support, mostly supplied by my younger sister, Nan, who lived nearby. She drove them to the grocery store and to doctor appointments, made sure they took their medications, accompanied them to church, and so much more. I traveled from my home in Virginia to Ohio as often as I could to help out and give Nan a break.

But eventually they needed even more care and supervision. Dementia was quickly progressing in my mother and father. Nan could no longer fulfill their needs while working a full-time job. So we prayerfully began to search for an assisted living community. There was a lot of angst during that time. My folks wanted to remain at home, although they knew they needed more support. We took them to visit a couple of potential places and explained why they needed to move. Some days they understood and agreed; other days they were steadfast about remaining in their beloved and familiar home. But after several years of these conversations, we the children made the decision and moved our parents to a nice assisted-living facility, much to their dismay. The adjustment period was difficult, but finally they settled in and enjoyed their new home.

After about a year, they had to move to the community's memory care unit. Dad soon passed away, leaving Mom alone after 62 years of marriage. Remarkably, she adjusted pretty well. Yet I was concerned about my mother's welfare and whether she was receiving the care and attention that she needed and deserved.

It has been a long time since Mom left me a voicemail. She's now 90 years old and doesn't call anymore. But I talk to her at least once a week via FaceTime when Nan visits her. Sometimes Mom doesn't recognize me, and I have to tell her that I am her oldest daughter and firstborn child. During our video visits, Mom is usually eating her favorite ice cream, coffee flavored, and most of the conversation is about the cute figurines she loves so much that line her TV stand. Whenever I tell her at the end of our chat that I love her and to "Be good"—which she often told us when we were youngsters—she responds, "OK," and reminds me I should do the same.

I miss the mother I used to talk to over the phone about all sorts of things. I pray every day that the Lord will watch over her. But I recognized something in that moment of hearing Mom's long-ago birthday voicemail: God's reassurance. Although my mother isn't the same as she used to be, she is still the mother who has been a blessing my entire life. As I listened to Mom's cheerful singing on the answering machine, God showed up to let me know that He will take care of Mom all the remaining days of her life. He is still with her. And He's with me, too. And if I ever forget, all I need to do is push play on my answering machine.

—*Barbranda Lumpkins Walls*

WHAT WILL YOU FIND?

Dig out a keepsake from a loved one—a letter, card, piece of jewelry, photo, or child's drawing. Remember the places you've been, times you've spent, and conversations you've had with that special person. Take a moment to thank God for the blessing this person has been to your life, and pray that you can bless someone else's life in the same way.

In My Scars

"But I will restore you to health and heal your wounds," declares the LORD.
—JEREMIAH 30:17 (NIV)

Running my fingers across the puckered scar, a wave of sensation washes over me—the skin is rough, a map of past battles, yet strangely comforting. The purple line, stark against my pale skin, speaks of a difficult surgery, a fight against a life-threatening illness.

Before my surgery, fear threatened to consume me. But amidst it, a flicker of hope sustained me, fueled by prayer and my faith community's unwavering support. Their love was a constant reminder I wasn't alone.

Now the scar is a vibrant echo of God's promise to His people in Jeremiah: "'But I will restore you to health and heal your wounds,' declares the LORD." God's healing touch wasn't just physical; He mended my emotional wounds as well. With every glance at the scar, I feel a surge of gratitude, warmth blooming in my chest—a testament to God's healing power, a constant whisper that "you are not broken."

This scar, a symbol of God's masterful stitching, is a second chance at life, a beautiful imperfection that whispers hope. It's a constant reminder of the strength I found in faith during that trial. God carried me through the darkest valley and I emerged stronger, the foundation of my faith more solid than ever.

Each touch whispers a prayer of thanks. This scar isn't just a physical mark; it's a badge of courage, a witness to the unwavering hope that held me fast during those difficult times. I am a tapestry of God's love and grace, a beautiful collection of imperfections murmuring resilience and ever-renewing faith.

—*Elly Gilbert*

WHAT WILL YOU FIND?

Do you have a physical reminder of a difficult time from the past? Perhaps it's a scar, or some type of memento. Touch it gently and remember how you met the challenge and overcame it. Offer a prayer of thanks to God for His healing power and the strength He provided.

Watching the Deer on the Wall

*As the deer pants for streams of water,
so my soul pants for you, my God.*
—**PSALM 42:1 (NIV)**

It was a battered oak picture frame, hidden under a table at a flea market, passed over by everyone walking by. It called my name, and I figured I could do something with it someday, maybe find a place for it at my old log cabin. I never imagined it would lead me to a new way of living.

It had once told the story of a church. A carved wooden square in the upper right corner declared, "Erected 1836." In the lower left corner, "Rebuilt 1900." Other carvings evoked the seasons of life, hope, and streams in the desert when hope could not be found.

That's the season I was in as I lay in a hospital bed in my home—installed temporarily while I was recovering from a traumatic fall—facing the story frame. Without knowing why, I'd backed the interior of the frame with a dark brown suede, then mounted a wooden deer head in the center. I'd encircled his neck with a leather strop of sleigh bells fit for a celebration—except in that moment I was far from a celebratory mood.

Confined to bed, my life on an agonizing pause, God seemed distant. Inaccessible. With nothing else to fix my eyes on, the wooden deer took on a life of its own. A verse I'd long ago memorized, but never lived, came alive as well.

As the deer pants for streams of water, so my soul pants for you, my God. It became my first thought on awakening, my last thought before closing my eyes. That longing for God brought Him to a desperate me.

I'm fully recovered now, the hospital bed long gone. In its place, hope. And so much to celebrate. Every morning and evening, I pause at that touchstone and remember. Repeat those dear life-giving words, my spirit brimming over with gratitude for the God who replenishes our spirits in life's deserts.

—*Roberta Messner*

WHAT WILL YOU FIND?

Take a gander around the place *you* call home. Is there a favorite object that brings to mind a promise from Scripture? Create a daily ritual of meditation that will bring water to your own parched places. Let it take you to a place of gratitude and celebration.

Holding a Red-Painted Spike

You were dead because of your sins and because your sinful nature was not yet cut away. Then God made you alive with Christ, for he forgave all our sins. He canceled the record of the charges against us and took it away by nailing it to the cross.
—COLOSSIANS 2:13-14 (NLT)

It's meant to be a memento, though it's not designed for display on a desk or shelf. I don't see it every day, though it's traveled with me from the Midwest to the South in four different homes across three different states. This dusty, gray, 8-inch spike with faded red paint sprayed on the bottom 3 inches is stored inside a wooden container in my home office.

I came across the spike again recently when my family was cleaning my office. Memories returned: A weekend church retreat with other new members. The organizers were intentional about creating a safe space for us to pour our pain out to each other, to share our own and carry the pain of others. As part of the closing ceremony, I was instructed to write down one thing I needed to "nail to the cross"—something that I wanted to eradicate from my life, which was symbolized by throwing the written paper into a fire-filled barrel. I was then directed to a small chapel where I could kneel and pray.

That weekend, I chose to nail procrastination to the cross and accept God's complete work in my life—that not only would He forgive my sins, but He also would relieve me of burdensome struggles. Before leaving the retreat, the organizers played the crucifixion scene from *The Passion of the Christ* to remind us of God's love and plan for us. They then gave each of the new members a spray-painted spike to remind us of His love and of the spiritual experiences we'd had that weekend.

It's always been hard for me to watch a crucifixion scene, or to think about the suffering that Jesus went through for our sake. Whenever I see that spike, it reminds me of the extreme love God showed me by sacrificing His only Son to bear my sins and to die on a cross in my place. Despite wickedness and weaknesses that attempt to trap me today, I know my past, present, and future sins and struggles were eradicated through God's redeeming love. I was forgiven then, and I am forgiven today.

—*Ericka Loynes*

WHAT WILL YOU FIND?

Draw a picture of a nail and write the words, "I am forgiven!" underneath. Add your personal touches to the final look and feel of the drawing. Hang it up in a prominent place as a daily reminder of how God has forgiven your sins and redeemed you. What other symbols represent His extreme love for you?

Sitting at the Pottery Wheel

Yet you, LORD, are our Father. We are the clay, you are the potter; we are all the work of your hand.
—ISAIAH 64:8 (NIV)

I sat at my pottery wheel alongside several other beginning ceramic students. Our stations formed a circle in the middle of a community art studio. My pound of clay wobbled under my hands as the wheel spun. Body bent over, I worked to center the clay, bringing it up and down with my hands until the wobble disappeared. The soft mound responded quickly to the pressure and direction I gave.

With the clay centered, I dipped my hands in the pail of water beside me. Then, overlapping the wet fingers of both hands, I pressed them deep into the middle of the mound, shaping the interior of what would become a small pot. With the proper depth established, it was time to pull up the walls.

As we worked, our instructor reminded us, "Always keep both hands on your clay." Starting at the base, with my left hand inside the cylinder and my right hand on the outside, I pressed my fingers in, moving them slowly up until my hands met at the top. The cylinder was taller now, but the walls still too thick. I returned my hands to the base and repeated the action.

"Keep both hands on your clay," the instructor said again. With those words, an image formed in my mind: God as the

Potter; me as the clay. Sitting at the pottery wheel, I felt His presence. I imagined His form bent over, His hands applying steady pressure and gentle direction. Sitting at the pottery wheel, I knew: *He keeps both hands on me.*

—*Kate Rietema*

WHAT WILL YOU FIND?

Visit a ceramic studio or watch a video clip of a potter on the Internet. Reflect back on specific situations when you've felt God's hands on you. Meditate on His faithfulness throughout the years. Then consider how He's shaping you now. Does the pressure of His hands feel uncomfortable? How can you respond in cooperation with His gentle direction?

In Grandma Currier's Quilt

The generous will themselves be blessed,
for they share their food with the poor.
—PROVERBS 22:9 (NIV)

God revealed the truth of this scripture through an incredible homemade quilt.

All of four-foot-nine-inches tall and hard of hearing, Grandma Currier was as full of vim and vinegar as anyone I know. She wasn't really my grandmother. We weren't even related. But 500 miles from home and attending a Christian high school with her real granddaughter, I felt privileged to be included in many a weekend in her home. She treated me as one of her own, with the same rights and responsibilities: respect the midnight curfew; do the dishes; sleep as late as desired on Saturday; attend church on Sunday; and don't tie up the phone. You wouldn't think such a tiny woman could be intimidating, but this was not a lady I wanted to tangle with, so I made sure to never break the rules.

Grandma Currier was famous for her homemade quilts. I especially admired the denim-patch quilts she created for each of her grandkids, every square embroidered with a unique picture. Years later, when my firstborn arrived, I received one of her appliquéd baby quilts, featuring the cutest bunny. I quickly declared it too beautiful for anything except hanging on the wall. There it presided over my second and third babies as well, providing a cozy atmosphere along with sweet memories for my bundles of love.

All too soon, my children outgrew baby decor, and the quilt was folded and relegated to a closet shelf. Then came a time of far-away war when Romanian orphans appeared in the media daily. News clips showed neglected children huddled together without the basics of survival. Feeling God's nudge, I put together a care package to send overseas with a local parent, who was traveling there to adopt a child. It seemed the least I could do. In an uncharacteristic act of generous abandon, I included Grandma Currier's beautiful baby quilt, imagining how special it might become to a needy child.

In the years that followed, I occasionally thought of that little quilt and regretted parting with it—especially the day I learned Grandma Currier had died. *It would be nice to own something to remember her by*, I thought—and then chastised myself for being so self-centered. *She would have loved knowing another child is happy because of her gift.*

Then, the unexpected happened.

I hadn't known that my in-laws were also recipients of a Grandma Currier quilt—a full-size one, big enough to serve as a bedspread on a double bed. On a visit to our home, they left the quilt with us, with instructions to return it to Grandma Currier's daughter, Donna. They thought she'd like to have it as a memory of her mother.

Before we had a chance to pass the quilt along, however, I received a call from Donna. "I hear you're holding one of my mom's quilts for me," she said. "But since I already have several, I wondered if you might like to keep it."

The quilt still graces our guest-room bed.

They say you can't out-give God. What do you suppose might happen if we ever really tried?

—*Terrie Todd*

WHAT WILL YOU FIND?

Is there something you own that you've been hanging on to, even though someone else might get more use out of it? Spend some time with that item, and listen for God's nudge. If He tells you it's time to let go, pay attention to what happens next. Is His generosity flowing back to you?

In the Ripples on the Water

May the Lord make your love increase and overflow for each other and for everyone else, just as ours does for you.
—1 THESSALONIANS 3:12 (NIV)

Usually, the sound of water lapping against the lakeshore settled my soul into a place of peace. But not today.

A morning email contained the news that my close friend, Joyce, was nearing the end of her battle with cancer. We had been friends for years, attending the same church where my husband was a pastor. Joyce's children had grown up with our children. Now we both had grandchildren.

I picked up a rock and threw it with all my strength into the water. I threw another rock. Then another.

"Jesus, what can I do for my friend?" I prayed. I felt so helpless at the unfairness of it all.

In the silence, I bent over and chose a flat, smooth stone. I palmed it in my hand. With a flick of the wrist, I let it fly.

One skip. Two. Three.

I watched the stone dance upon the surface of the water. Every touch became a ripple. The circles spread out wider and wider, until the entire lake was alive with movement. As I watched the ripples, I heard the answer to my prayerful question.

You can love her children's children.

I bowed my head, grateful for this hope-filled direction. With those words, I realized I was *not* helpless.

Joyce's grandchildren were signed up to attend our church's music camp the following week. As a teacher at the camp, I could love her grandchildren and continue the legacy my friend had begun. Joyce's influence would not end. The ripples of her life would spread in ever-widening circles.

—Lynne Hartke

WHAT WILL YOU FIND?

Go to a body of water and select a flat stone. Palm it in your hand. With a flick of the wrist, let it fly. Watch it dance upon the surface of the water. Take time and reflect on the ripple-effect of your life. How have your actions impacted others? How have others sent their ripples into your life? As you ponder the spreading circles, listen. What is God saying to you?

At a Family Picnic

Be devoted to one another in love. Honor one another above yourselves.
—ROMANS 12:10 (NIV)

Among my favorite pastimes are drives in the country for family picnics. Though my husband, David, and I often pack lunch and travel to scenic areas, the rare opportunities spent at a park with our daughter and son-in-law are priceless.

Those mornings, I fill our basket with an assortment of salads, sandwich fixings, and sweet treats, knowing full well my daughter is in her own kitchen doing the same, and that we will have ample food—enough for several meals. We meet at the park and spread the tablecloth at a table or grassy spot. Relaxing in the shade of an old oak or mighty pine, munching on delectable tidbits, we catch up on each other's lives. The air is sweet with our closeness.

On one such day, I was returning from a visit to the restroom, and I saw my loved ones as if in a snapshot. My son-in-law was smiling at something my daughter said as my husband took photos of the woodsy surroundings. And there, in the midst of our joy, laughter, and peace, I saw God. He was in the glorious trees dotting the lawn and the sunshine on our backs. He was in the juicy peaches and the spicy iced tea, the exuberance of children at play nearby. His affection filled the glances I shared with my daughter and the hugs my husband offered. He is love, and life abundant, and He was there—is still here, with us and in us—taking part in every moment, making it His.

—Heidi Gaul

WHAT WILL YOU FIND?

Set aside a day to visit a nearby park with loved ones. Invite them to bring a dish, an outdoor game, and an open heart. Be prepared to spot God amid the spills, the smiles, and the laughter, and to feel His love in the hugs.

In a Yellow Butterfly

And we all, who with unveiled faces contemplate the Lord's glory, are being transformed into his image with ever-increasing glory, which comes from the Lord, who is the Spirit.
—2 CORINTHIANS 3:18 (NIV)

I was a mess. Poor decision after poor decision left me as a young, single mom with limited resources and a broken heart. I reached for God and His people through a divorce recovery retreat.

The women there met me right where I was and loved me, helping me on a path toward Jesus. They taught me about His character and His grace. Using the butterfly to illustrate the process of our spiritual growth and transformation, they placed yellow butterflies on our doors, on our notebooks, in our rooms. They reminded us of the journey for the caterpillar and how we, too, can be transformed as we allow God to shape our lives.

During the final session, I poured my heart out to God at the makeshift altar. It felt as though I was tearing out of the grasp of grief and loss. In my mind's eye, I set my broken choices at His feet and felt my heart begin to heal. Just like the caterpillar wrapped in silky darkness, the transformation process was uncomfortable. Yet such beauty as God healed and restored my wounded heart!

Radically touched by God's grace through the love of His people, I began to grow and mature and flourish. Today, the butterfly is a constant reminder of God's faithfulness for me. In the highs, in the lows, in the daily stuff of life, whenever a yellow butterfly dances by, I feel God's deep and abiding love. I settle into His faithfulness and remember how He transformed this caterpillar heart into the spirit of a soaring butterfly.

—*Elsa Kok Colopy*

WHAT WILL YOU FIND?

Life is painful. Circumstances squeeze and shape and mold us. What was a particularly difficult time in your life that faith helped you through? Is there an object or symbol, like a butterfly, that represents that time for you? Seek it out today, and remember the beauty that came from the hardship.

As Ginkgo Leaves Fell

As far as the east is from the west, so far has he removed our transgressions from us.
—PSALM 103:12 (NIV)

Past sins slither in our minds, attempting to suffocate peace when least expected, and birthdays are not immune. As my husband and I made our way to Carl Sandburg's home, the first stop on my birthday weekend, the peaceful winding roads leading to Flat Rock, North Carolina, starkly contrasted with the unrest in my heart.

It began while driving our four young grandchildren back home from a visit the day before. They asked about their daddy as a little boy, which of course also led to a discussion about their grandfather, my ex-husband. The youngest, age 5, struggled to connect the dots. "You were married to Grandpa?"

Glancing at her in the rearview mirror, her innocent confusion convicted me all over again. Long before I accepted Jesus into my heart and life, I had left their grandfather for another man, one I later ended up divorcing. The memories revived a coil of shame and condemnation that was hard to make straight, even after all these years. It haunted me after we dropped off the children and I was still wrestling with it during that birthday drive. By faith, I believe Christ forgave my sins and washed me clean from all unrighteousness, but truth and feelings battled it out all the way to the Connemara parking lot.

As we strolled up the long, meandering path leading to Sandburg's home, my feet felt as heavy as my heart. I was weary from the mental tug-of-war, but, like a good Southerner, I smiled and stuffed my emotions down a little deeper with each step. On Sandburg's front porch, a guide from another tour asked everyone nearby to stop and observe a nearby ginkgo tree, because there were hints that the golden, fan-shaped leaves were preparing to drop.

Suddenly, right in front of our eyes, every leaf trickled down simultaneously. One minute, the tree was full of golden, fan-shaped leaves, and the next, they were a carpet on the ground underneath bare branches.

Of the 44,640 minutes in October, God placed me front and center for a once-a-year shedding ginkgo tree. I struggled to hold back tears as I stood in amazement at this glorious visual that clearly demonstrated what He did with my sin and shame at the moment of salvation. He dropped it. Not little by little, but at once, He removed my sin as far as the east is from the west. In that moment, I felt how deeply God pays attention to my heart.

I arrived at Carl Sandburg's home wounded and bound by shame from a sin that led to the division of our family decades earlier, but I left a free woman, wholly convinced of God's grace.

Now, when shame attempts to slink its way into my heart, I refuse its entry, knowing there is no condemnation for those in Christ Jesus (Romans 8:1). When I pray, I draw near with confidence, assured that mercy and grace await (Hebrews 4:16). And I walk in freedom because no one wants us to experience freedom more than God, proven by Christ, who hung on a tree, died, and was raised to life so that the curse of sin may fall once and for all.

—Cathy Baker

WHAT WILL YOU FIND?

I purchased a small ginkgo tree to plant in my yard as a visual celebration of that moment with God. Consider planting a flower, plant, or tree in your yard or planter to remind you of a specific time God "spoke" to you, and you listened.

In a Social Media Memory

He who began a good work in you will carry it on to completion until the day of Christ Jesus.
—PHILIPPIANS 1:6 (NIV)

Social media has a unique blend of pros and cons. One of its most endearing features is its ability to evoke memories. As I scroll through the "On This Day" feature, I'm transported back to moments that are etched in my heart, reminding me of God's unwavering faithfulness and provision. I'm able to revisit the precious moments of my now-grown children's younger days, and in doing so, I'm reminded how God has lovingly shaped their paths.

This morning, a familiar face popped up in my social media memories—my son, Jack, no more than 7 years old, sprawled at the kitchen table. Books were scattered before him, supposedly the tools of a studious afternoon. But a mischievous glint in his eye and a telltale twist of his body betrayed his true focus.

"What are you doing?" I asked, a smile tugging at my lips. His answer, delivered with a nonchalant shrug but a serious tone: "Oh, just thinkin' about God and the world and stuff."

Every time I look at that photo, I remember the way that answer tickled me—and brought me into an acute awareness of God's provision. *Jack will grow and mature,* He whispered to my heart, *but I will always be with him.*

Over a decade has passed, yet I still catch that same faraway look in my son's eye. Jack has grown into a young man who continues to ponder life's profound questions and is deeply committed to representing Christ in the world. His innate curiosity about God and the universe remains a spark that—as I'm reminded whenever I see those old photos—will continue to illuminate his path throughout his life.

—*Elly Gilbert*

WHAT WILL YOU FIND?

Take a few moments today to revisit the past. Open your favorite social media app and scroll through your "On This Day" memories. Flip through the pages of an old photo album. As you encounter these memories, recall God's faithfulness to you. Don't just skim—pause, reflect, and savor the details.

In the Ties that Bind

*Tie them as symbols on your hands
and bind them on your foreheads.*
—DEUTERONOMY 6:8 (NIV)

I'd only been a VA nurse a few weeks when I was assigned to change a big post-op abdominal dressing. My patient was a successful businessman in town; he'd chosen our hospital because of our reputation for veteran-centered care. *There's nothing to be nervous about,* I told myself as I gathered the supplies. *No one knows you've had that tumor removed from your head.* I'd hidden my surgical bruises behind makeup and glasses and put on a wig to cover my shaved head and roadmap of stitches, but I still felt exposed. I didn't want anyone to see my scars.

I'd medicated my patient for pain, but his face grimaced as he braced himself for the unknowns of his first dressing change. Then the unthinkable happened. As I leaned over his wound, my wig with its frosted curls fell off my stubbly scalp. I was beyond mortified. As I reached for my wig, aghast, I felt my patient's hand over mine, patting it softly.

When his wife visited that afternoon, she had a gift he'd asked her to bring: a paisley-patterned tie he'd worn on his first job interview. The prospective boss had taken him to a buffet for lunch. During the interview, he'd leaned over the soup and sopped the silk. His wife had gotten the stain out, but he'd kept the tie to remind himself to accept his own mistakes with grace. He got the job, by the way, and it became a stepping stone to him owning his own business.

His tie became a reminder to me, too. Throughout my 38-year VA nursing career, patients in that community of caring heard that I collected ties from patients and began gifting me with ties they no longer needed because they retired from a job, downsized a home or closet, or upsized to heaven. As word got around, a few who weren't my patients even brought them to me, sharing their stories about why they no longer needed them. I tacked skinny and wide ones of every color and design to bulletin boards, and even trimmed an office lampshade with them.

These days, they adorn the hem of a denim pencil skirt I wear when I speak to veteran's groups. The ties that forever bind our hearts, reminding me of all the times that I saw God in my patients, through their kindness, endurance, and generous spirits.

—Roberta Messner

WHAT WILL YOU FIND?

Is there an object of clothing that *you* cherish? One with a memory connected to a special one or reminiscent of a time and place? Look for a way to enjoy it in your home or to wear it—and be open to the ways that you can share its story with others.

In Dappled Sunlight

When Jesus spoke again to the people, he said, "I am the light of the world. Whoever follows me will never walk in darkness, but will have the light of life."
—JOHN 8:12 (NIV)

Dappled sunlight danced across the conference table, filtering through the window behind me, mesmerizing me. I'd never sat in that seat at my Bible study class, usually preferring a place closer to the door where I could easily escape if I felt uncomfortable. I was afraid someone would get a glimpse of the real me and realize I didn't belong in this group of godly women. I felt sure my dark and sinful past disqualified me from being one of these faithful women of God, just as the dark spots in the dappled sunlight dimmed its brilliance.

But that day, after several months studying God's Word, I felt brave. Not one of my fellow Bible study ladies had judged me, and I had begun to feel at home among them. I chose a seat on the far side of the table, away from the door. A seat in the sun. As I watched the swirling spots of sunlight on the table in front of me, I sensed God moving in my heart, telling me that His Light revealed everything about me—everything I had ever done or said or thought, every single sin—and He loved me despite it all. He loved me enough to die for me on the Cross. The darkness of my past didn't disqualify me from serving Him just as the dark spots swirling within the dappled sunlight didn't diminish the sun. Rather, it made me perfectly fit to understand the depth of His love.

Now when I see dappled sunlight streaming through a window or dancing below the wind-rustled leaves of a tree, I am reminded of that moment in the Bible study room when I finally saw my worth in God's eyes. Even when discouraging words or thoughts try to obscure His light, the truth that He loves me makes its way through to dance like dappled sunlight in my heart.

—*Linda L. Kruschke*

WHAT WILL YOU FIND?

Find a piece of lace and hold it up loosely in front of a sunny window to create dappled light on the floor or a table. Notice how the light moves to cover every part of the surface, even when some parts are in shadow. Can you see how God's light reveals His great love for you?

Seeing a Statue of Jesus

He withdrew about a stone's throw beyond them, knelt down and prayed, "Father, if you are willing, take this cup from me; yet not my will, but yours be done."
—LUKE 22:41-42 (NIV)

In the middle of my university campus stood a small stone prayer chapel. Heavy wooden doors opened to tile floors, wooden pews, and stained-glass windows.

The chapel itself was reverent and quiet, but at the front there was a statue I didn't like. It depicted Jesus draped over a rock, face etched in anguish, a goblet in His hand. It was meant to represent Luke 22:42 (NIV): "Father, if you are willing, take this cup from me." But when I first saw it, it didn't feel comforting; the image felt cold and unsettling. I would have chosen Jesus smiling, perhaps holding a lamb or surrounded by children.

Nearly every morning before classes began, I slipped through those heavy wooden doors and sat alone in a pew to pray—halfway down the aisle, on the left. My four years at this university were at times wonderful, and at times difficult and lonely. But finally, after a hundred mornings in the pew on the left, staring at the statute, I finally understood. No one knew the emotional discomfort I felt—except Jesus. I looked at Him, saw the anguish on His face as if for the first time, and I knew: *Jesus understood.* I was not alone in my pain. Finally, the statue brought me comfort.

It's been 25 years since I first slipped through those doors as a lonely and timid freshman, but even now, I am comforted by that image of Jesus. He faced immense hardship. He understands suffering, and He can empathize with us—whatever our difficult situation. Because Jesus faced suffering, we are never alone in ours.

—*Kate Rietema*

WHAT WILL YOU FIND?

Read Luke 22:39–44. Close your eyes and imagine this scene of Jesus. What must He have felt in that moment? Jesus didn't need to endure suffering, but for our sake, He did. Write a prayer detailing something in your life that has brought—or still brings—you pain. Feel Him beside you, and know that you are never alone.

CHAPTER 6

finding God in nature

In a Sudden Caribbean Rain

For God alone, O my soul, wait in silence,
for my hope is from him.
—PSALM 62:5 (ESV)

Nighttime on an out-of-the-way Caribbean coast. My hotel room was a wooden building on stilts—it's hurricane country there, complete with flooding storm surges. I took a guitar out onto the porch and sat on a weathered deck chair next to an ashtray filled with some previous guest's cigarette butts. I listened to the ocean, watched the lights of passing ships, and strummed John Prine songs (it was a Prine type of night). Around midnight it started to rain. And not just any rain. Biblical stuff. Thunder on the old tin roof. I stopped playing and listened.

I felt Him then. I love the way He comes that way, so completely unexpected, letting me know not only that He's there but that it's *His* idea. I mumbled my thanks for such a beautiful night and His beautiful comfort.

The rain lessened, fading to a light patter. I breathed in, loving the smell of the rain and even more the feeling of being close to my Creator. I strummed again. I worshiped in my heart. *Make me an angel that flies from Montgomery*... Not necessarily doctrinally correct, but the sentiment was there.

It's funny, somehow that night stands out to me as one of the great worship experiences of my life. I wasn't singing hymns or praise songs. There was certainly no sound system, no mood lighting, stage, or even building. Just me, John Prine, the rain, and Jesus.

The sun shone bright the next morning. Much more Buffet than Prine. I smiled as I headed down the road, refreshed. Washed clean by Caribbean rain, buoyed by the presence of Jesus—my traveling companion, my Lord.

—*Buck Storm*

WHAT WILL YOU FIND?

Do you ever pay attention to the rain? Next time it storms, turn off your electronic devices and listen to the sound of the wind and the water. Let your mind dwell with the God who made the rain, and worship in whatever way feels best to you.

Looking Up at an Eclipse

The heavens declare the glory of God; the skies proclaim the work of his hands.
—PSALM 19:1 (NIV)

I was standing in an unfamiliar place atop a sandy hill, and I didn't know what to expect in the coming moments. I had never seen a solar eclipse from a totality zone.

It wasn't only the next half-hour that held mystery, but the coming months. Days before, my husband and I and our three-going-on-four children had sold our home, packed up our travel trailer, and headed west to the Pacific Ocean for a 9-week road trip. A lot felt uncertain in that season. My husband had quit his job, and we were without an income or home address. With a safety net of savings stored away in a bank account and a meager remnant of belongings we'd tucked away in storage, we'd hit the road. A sense of excitement filled our conversations and, along with it, some looming doubts and questions. The future was obscured in fog. Would the trip bring clarity around what we wanted for our young family? What would we do when we returned to our community, found a new home, and my husband began building his own business? Would we have any money left? I tried to subdue worry and open my heart and mind to what God might have for us. The horizon was full of possibilities, and it felt fitting to begin our adventure with this display of cosmic splendor.

Just before ten in the morning, the warm August air began to plummet in temperature. The fog, which had been meandering out of the surrounding bay and over ocean waters, reversed and started rushing back in around us. Seagulls shouted in confusion from the piers. Sea lions joined them, barking in pandemonium as the sun began to disappear. I was determined not to succumb with the animals to fear or chaos, but to trust that sometimes it's in the most uncertain moments when God whispers a promise into our hearts.

As the moon moved directly between the Earth and the sun, extinguishing light and transforming the morning sky into night, my mind stilled. I held my breath.

"How does God do that?" my four-year-old son asked in astonishment.

I wondered the same thing as I craned my neck upward. Stars shone in the dark sky as day turned into night. And yet, I knew that what seemed utterly unnatural was, in fact, entirely natural. When God strung together the cosmos at creation, He dialed in systems, math, and gravity to choreograph the unbelievable scene before us. I heard Him whisper to my heart that in the same way, He'd planned well in advance for this season in my family's life. Whatever felt out-of-control and unscripted was indeed within His sovereign and powerful control.

As the moon continued its voyage, a sliver of sunlight broke through and began to drench the horizon in light again. Sunlight gushed across the sky, and the animals resumed their routines. But I would not return to normal.

Standing beneath the sky as light chased away the darkness, I thought back to Abraham staring up into the stars in Hebron. How many times had I read his story in Genesis 15? Yet never until this day had it seemed so profound: God making a covenant, an everlasting promise with a man in an unfamiliar land who had an uncertain future. In Genesis 15:5 (NIV), I'd read that God "took him outside and said, 'Look up at the sky and count the stars—if indeed you can count them.' Then he said to him, 'So shall your offspring be.'"

God had brought Abraham out beneath an expanse of stars and anchored His promise in the visual of the sky. In much the same way, God was rooting His promise in my heart and mind through the total eclipse experience. Like Abraham, I couldn't yet see what lay ahead or where the road might take my family. But as God brought me outside and solidified His promise through an unforgettable visual, I had the confidence to move forward.

As our journey took us along the ocean and through forests, then finally back home to a new beginning, God assured me time and again, whenever I looked up into the sky, that He was with us each step, and nothing was uncertain to Him.

—*Eryn Lynum*

WHAT WILL YOU FIND?

Watch a rainbow or stand beneath the sky during a full moon, sunset, or sunrise. Ask God about your future, and allow Him to reassure your heart. Like Abraham looking up into the stars, know that God has great things in store and will lead you along the way.

Following the Red Dirt Road

Blessed are all who fear the Lord, who walk in obedience to him. You will eat the fruit of your labor; blessings and prosperity will be yours.
—PSALM 128:1–2 (NIV)

Irises are my favorite flowers. The colors and varieties seem endless, a testament to God's creativity. I have at least ten varieties in my yard, purple being the most common. But my favorite is a bearded iris called Red Dirt Road. Its deep shade of burgundy blends beautifully with the peach center and purple caterpillar-like beard.

A few years ago, my husband dug up my Red Dirt Road rhizomes to make room for a lace hydrangea that was getting too much sun. At about the same time, he dug up and thinned an overcrowded patch of purple irises. The next year, my Red Dirt Road didn't bloom. I asked him where he replanted them. He couldn't remember. I'd just have to wait until they bloomed again.

Two years passed without a single red iris in my yard. I had almost given up hope I'd ever see them again. Then one day, as we packed up the car for a trip, I noticed something odd in the patch of purple irises at the end of our driveway. Was it . . . ? It was! A beautiful Red Dirt Road beginning to unfurl. Two more buds waited to open in the coming days.

It hit me then, standing next to that patch of purple irises: the way that God knows every detail of our lives—even the location of a missing flower—and He doesn't want us to lose hope. When we think something is lost, when we aren't even looking for it anymore, he brings it to us out of the blue (or in this case, purple). And although iris season is over, come next spring that Red Dirt Road will remind me of the beauty He has in store for my future.

—*Linda L. Kruschke*

WHAT WILL YOU FIND?

Stroll through a beautiful flower garden and take time to notice the variety of colors, shapes, and sizes of the blooms you see. Does one stand out to you as especially lovely? Find out what type it is, and when it blooms. What had to happen in order for you to be here at just that time to see it? What other unexpected blessings do you sense God preparing for you?

On a Morning Walk through the Vineyard

*"I am the vine; you are the branches....
Apart from me you can do nothing."*
—JOHN 15:5 (NIV)

I enjoy working in my vineyard in the early morning—walking the rows, inspecting the grape clusters, thinning the vines with my pruning knife. This morning the dew glints on the trellis wires like fairy lights, and curlicue green tendrils stretch out from the vines, reaching for something to cling to. Up ahead I see a cluster of leaves all droopy and dry, and I know right away what the problem is. Sure enough, the branch has become separated from the vine. No life-giving nutrition is reaching the leaves; they will soon wither and go brown. There will be no fruit. Separated from the source of its life, the branch is already dead, but doesn't know it yet.

Walking along, swinging the pruning knife in an easy rhythm, I find myself thinking about my life, and how, lately, my high ideals and noble aspirations keep withering on the vine. My Bible study time keeps getting pushed aside by worldly concerns. I neglect my prayers. I entertain thoughts that are angry, vengeful, vain. I allow all manner of evil to go prancing through my mind. I produce precious little fruit. I know what the problem is: the branch has become separated from the vine.

The wind comes whispering down the rows, ruffling the leaves, and I hear in my heart the words of Christ: *I am the vine; you are the branches.* I cannot reattach my grape branches once they have separated from the vine; what's done is done. But I can reattach myself, heart and soul, to my Savior, and I do.

—*Louis Lotz*

WHAT WILL YOU FIND?

Look at the grapes on your next trip to the grocery store. Imagine the woody vine from which the cluster grew, providing it with life-giving nutrition. Are you bearing fruit in your life? Stand still, and listen for what God might be whispering to you . . .

Using a Bird ID App

I praise you, for I am fearfully and wonderfully made. Wonderful are your works; my soul knows it very well.
—PSALM 139:14 (ESV)

The bird call app on my phone solved the mystery.
 I was listening to the songbirds while I enjoyed the sunset view from my deck. Two different sounds coming from the same spot in the backyard puzzled me. I heard high-pitched whistles that sounded like "cheer, cheer, cheer," followed by a series of two-syllable notes. One type of bird or two?

I opened the bird call app and clicked on the sound button. The digital recording matched both sounds to the same bird and displayed a picture and the name of the species—northern cardinal. Peering up at a tall snowball shrub, I saw the familiar sight of the handsome red bird perched near the top. Both sounds were part of his repertoire.

I left the app open, and soon photos of a Carolina wren and a brown thrasher popped up on my phone, followed by a robin, a house finch, and a mockingbird. The app highlighted the name of each bird when it soloed. Fascinated, I listened to the pitches and cadences of the various species and tried to spot each one as it called. So many different birds in such a small area!

The array of changing photos reminded me how God, the Creator of our feathered friends, made each of them unique. Like the birds, our appearance, voice, and purpose vary. God gave each person their own unique gifts to bless others—sending cards of encouragement, contributing time or money, or serving in practical ways. How often had I compared myself to others, wishing I could do what they did? *And how dull would your backyard be,* God whispered, *if every bird sounded exactly the same?*

I thanked God for the gifts I have and the way I can use them to honor Him and meet the needs of people He sends my way.

—Jeannie Waters

WHAT WILL YOU FIND?

Install a bird call app on your phone and spend time outdoors. Notice the songs and flight patterns of various birds. As the app identifies the species you hear, take a moment to appreciate how each one is unique. Thank God for your own uniqueness and ask Him to show you how to use your gifts to serve His purpose.

In Tiny Spiral Shells

There before me lies the mighty ocean, teeming with life of every kind, both great and small.
—PSALM 104:25 (TLB)

It was a surreally perfect day on New Zealand's North Island. The Tasman Sea mirrored the azure of a cloudless sky, stretching west 1,300 miles toward the coast of Australia. Massive waves danced up and down the black sands of Piha Beach to the thundering soundtrack of the incoming tide. I stood in the shadow of Lion's Rock, awestruck into silence. I was so immersed in the rugged landscape of volcanic rock and fern-covered cliffs that I almost missed the miniature miracles that lay at my feet.

Thankfully, I'm a grandmother of five. Whenever I travel, I try to bring home a souvenir for each of my grandchildren. Being too thrifty to purchase a soon-to-be-discarded trinket at a local gift shop, I decided to search for shells. But instead of the usual cockles, clam shells, and chunks of coral I'd picked up for my grandchildren in other parts of the world, this beach was littered with small spirals. The almost translucent ivory swirls, less than an inch in diameter, made the beach look like an inverted night sky, with spiral galaxies strewn in abundance across the glittering black sand.

Enchanted by God's boundless creativity, I filled my pockets with the tiny treasures. I knew my grandchildren would be just as delighted as I was by my find. But as a local guide described what I held in my hand, my jaw literally dropped in amazement. This coiled shell was from a ram's horn squid. Although I enjoy learning about all of God's odd creatures, this was one I'd never heard of before. Now it's one I'll never forget.

I learned that we know more about this cephalopod's shell than we do about the creature itself. Although the squid's shell was categorized in 1758 and has been studied ever since, the tiny squid wasn't seen in its natural habitat until 2020. One reason for this is that it's only about 3 inches long and lives between 1,000 and 3,000 feet beneath the ocean's surface. In the dark waters at this depth, this amazing little critter even has a tiny taillight, which is believed to be used to blind prey or predators.

The tiny shells I collected are the squid's buoyancy organ. When they are alive, this coil is filled with a kind of oil. A bubble in this fluid helps the squid sink or rise in the water. Although encountering a ram's horn squid is extremely rare, their shells are quite common and are found in tropical and subtropical beaches around the world.

Back in my hotel room, holding one of those mathematically perfect white spirals in my hand, I had a profound sense of how big God is, and how small my own brain is in comparison. There is near-infinite detail that goes into the workings of the world, and He designed it all, down to the most minute processes, down to a tiny little squid that goes practically unnoticed in the vast complexity of God's wild, wonderful creation.

As I carefully packed these delicate little ram's horn squid shells into my luggage to take home to my grandchildren, I realized that I was giving each of them a psalm they could hold in their hands—written not in words, but in God's design. Each miraculous little shell sang a song of praise to its Creator through its intricacy, artistry, and innovation. Now, every time my grandchildren look at these "common" shells, their wonder will revive an echo of praise that continually resounds from all God has made.

—*Vicki Kuyper*

WHAT WILL YOU FIND?

Take a walk outside, anywhere along a dirt path or nature trail. Pause intentionally every so often and look down. What little miracles can you find at your feet? What is the shape of them, the weight? How do they reflect the beauty and complexity of life itself, unnoticed by the people who pass by? Ask God to help you more readily see the tiny wonders that surround you each and every day.

In a Field of Daffodils

"If God cares so wonderfully for flowers that are here today and gone tomorrow, won't he more surely care for you?"
—MATTHEW 6:30 (TLB)

The early spring sun felt warm on my back as I walked down the dusty path. My family ran ahead, enjoying the freedom of fresh air after a long winter of cold and snow. As they rounded the corner ahead, I heard them chatter excitedly, calling me to hurry and see. I tried to guess what was ahead—maybe a cool rock or a bunny in the field. When I caught up and saw what they were excited about, I was speechless.

A field of daffodils spread out before us. Bright yellows mixed with creamy soft yellows surrounded by vibrant green stems, filling the landscape. It was a stunning display of spring beauty. Wanting to be part of it, my kids carefully tiptoed through the flowers, finding little places to sit and admire them. Instinctively, I grabbed my phone to capture the memory and the beauty.

I flipped through the pictures as my kids basked in the floral display. Looking at the pictures, the daffodils were stunning. But they were no match for the beauty I saw in my kids. I saw how their faces lit with joy and how their eyes sparkled. The flowers faded into a lovely backdrop to display what was even more important.

In that moment, I understood how God sees me. Even in the most beautiful places surrounded by the most beautiful things, God sees *my* beauty. My smile and my eyes stand out to Him among all the beauty of His creation. As beautiful as the flowers are, God sees me and cares for me even more.

—*Rebecca Hastings*

WHAT WILL YOU FIND?

Think of the most beautiful place you've ever seen. Picture it in your mind. Now consider how God sees the same scene. He notices all the beauty you see, and still, His eyes fall on you. Imagine the smile that spreads across His face as He says, "You, my child, are so beautiful."

In a Bag of Compost

And provide for those who grieve in Zion—to bestow on them a crown of beauty instead of ashes, the oil of joy instead of mourning, and a garment of praise instead of a spirit of despair.
—ISAIAH 61:3 (NIV)

I was tired. Weary. Worn out. It had been an incredibly difficult season, and I didn't have the energy to do much of anything. I knew I needed to get out of my own head, so I ventured out one spring morning to purchase some flowers for our pots.

There's something therapeutic about dumping out the old, dried-up flower stems and roots, filling our pots with good soil and planting beautiful flowers into the fresh dirt. In some sweet way, it reminds me that winter is over and summer is just around the corner.

On this particular spring day, I had picked up a sale item, an especially odiferous bag of natural fertilizer. I opened the bag and nearly gagged. Full of manure and "natural" compost, it guaranteed that flowers would flourish once the roots were nurtured by its smelly nutrients. I had to laugh as, in a sudden flash of insight, the Holy Spirit applied that beautiful truth to my recent circumstances.

Yes, it had been one of the hardest seasons of my life. Yes, the pain and turmoil had been nearly more than I could bear. But I could see, even though I was still weary, that I had grown. My dependence on Jesus was deeper, my pride and defenses broken down, my awareness of small gifts and pleasure increased. He was forging something beautiful in my life through these deep valleys and I couldn't help but be grateful. Just like that stinky, disgusting manure producing the most vibrant of flowers, it was this most stinky journey that was growing me into something refined and beautiful as well.

—*Elsa Kok Colopy*

WHAT WILL YOU FIND?

Have you ever tried composting, or used compost when planting something? Perhaps driven by a field that was fertilized using manure? The next time you're outside, put your fingers in the earth and think about the odiferous circumstances that have shaped your world—the things that had to decay in order to fuel new growth. Nothing is wasted as our God uses every bit of our heartache to make us look more like Him—vibrant, colorful, enthralling.

On a Freeway North of Santa Barbara

*Surely goodness and mercy shall follow me all the days of my life, and I shall dwell in the house of the L*ORD *forever.*
—PSALM 23:6 (ESV)

Just north of Santa Barbara, the freeway jogged west. My tires hummed as the Great Artist busied Himself with the sunset. The October kind. Deep burnt orange fading to purple, silhouetting the trees and telephone poles in sharp relief. I wish I could say I noticed His work immediately, but I can't. I don't remember what I was thinking about, but it wasn't Him.

Until it was.

It's funny, that's the way it's always been with us. One second I'm mindlessly unaware, just another knucklehead rolling down life's highway, the next He is there, emphatic and unrelenting.

Maybe the sunset was a subconscious trigger, but I honestly doubt there was any profundity on my part. Because I know me and I know Him. *Because* of me, it is *always* Him. Whether I'd marked the calendar or not, He and I had an appointment. Zoned out, lost in my own thoughts, in an instant that orange sky exploded into my vision. And with it, an overwhelming sense of my future.

IN NATURE

For lack of better words—I honestly wish I had them—I was filled with a profound sense of *heaven,* and it became more real than anything in this physical world. I was flooded with a sense of peace I've rarely felt since.

I don't know why it happened that day, that time, and not the day before or the day after. It's been nearly 30 years now. A whole lot of sunsets have come and gone, but I remember that one like yesterday. I truly believe God gave me an unsolicited gift. A beautiful glimpse into our imminent reality. One planned for us before He breathed this world into existence. I'm so grateful. I'll carry it with me always.

At least until the day I lay it back at His feet.

—*Buck Storm*

WHAT WILL YOU FIND?

There's a sunset every day, but we don't always take the time to appreciate it. Pick a day when you feel stress, or when God feels far away, and go to a spot where you can get a good view of the sunset—a wide-open space, or somewhere high up. Watch, and let yourself dwell on the glorious future that awaits.

Watching the Hummingbirds

"Where is God... who teaches us more than he teaches the beasts of the earth and makes us wiser than the birds in the sky?"
—JOB 35:10-11 (NIV)

A hummingbird feeder hangs outside my office window. It is one of five that my husband maintains throughout the year. He makes fresh nectar with granulated sugar and water every week. When he refills them, he washes each feeder with hot soapy water, scrubbing the feeding ports with a tiny chenille brush. He works hard to provide for our local Anna's hummingbirds, which don't migrate south in winter.

If the feeder outside my window runs low, I know because a hummingbird will hover at the window and glare at me as if to say, "Hey, tell that guy who fills the feeders to quit loafing around and give us more food!"

An interesting fact about Anna's hummingbirds is that they are territorial about their food sources. Each feeder has its resident bully who chases the other birds away. This is true even if there is also an abundance of flowers for them to eat from, which is the case in our yard from spring through fall.

Watching the activity at the feeder one day, I wondered, *How much are we like those hummingbirds?* God gives us all we need, and yet sometimes, like the hovering hummingbird, we complain. We grumble that there might not be enough if what we have runs low. Like the bully, we sometimes guard what we have instead of sharing it with others. *Do I do that too?*

Now when I see those hummingbirds at the feeder, it's a reminder to pray: to guard myself against worry and selfishness, and instead focus on drinking the sweet nectar of God's care and provision, lovingly provided each day.

—*Linda L. Kruschke*

WHAT WILL YOU FIND?

Consider hanging a hummingbird feeder in your yard or on your apartment balcony. As you watch the small hovering birds feed, remember God's provision. Is there a need you are worrying about, unsure if He will provide? Watch and listen as He reassures you of His constant presence and care.

At the End of the Fog

You alone are the Lord. *You made the heavens, even the highest heavens, and all their starry host, the earth and all that is on it, the seas and all that is in them. You give life to everything, and the multitudes of heaven worship you.*
—NEHEMIAH 9:6 (NIV)

Preparing to go home after having dinner at a friend's house, my family and I stepped outside and into a thick canopy of fog. The sun was below the horizon as we climbed into our car, and we could hardly see 10 feet in front of us. And yet, 10 minutes later, as we neared our neighborhood, the fog disappeared. A moment before, we were nearly blind. Now the sky spread out before us, a crystal-clear expanse shimmering with stars. A bright flash lit the sky, and my husband and I gasped.

"You saw that?" I asked him.

"I saw it."

A moment later, another streak of light traveled across the horizon.

"Are they meteors?" I asked. He stayed silent, watching the sky. I pulled out my phone, and the Internet quickly confirmed a meteorite shower was taking place that evening.

We drove right past our street and onto a hill outside of town, where our family stood beneath the night sky and watched lights dancing across the expanse in the form of meteorites. It was difficult to believe that we hadn't been able to glimpse the sky minutes before. Now we were witnessing an awe-inspiring display of the Creator's design.

Standing under the shooting stars, God reminded me that darkness never wins—His light always breaks through the fog. Whether we're being slowed down by obscured dreams, an uncertain future, or unanswered prayers, His light will illuminate the way ahead, revealing the unfathomable beauty of His design.

—*Eryn Lynum*

WHAT WILL YOU FIND?

Drive away from city lights and sit beneath a starry sky, watch a full moon rise, or enjoy a sunrise. As you do, consider how God's light always shatters darkness, and reflect on the ways He has pushed darkness back in your life with the light of His love.

CHAPTER 7

finding God in loved ones

In a White Cardboard Box

*The LORD has done great things for us,
and we are filled with joy.*
—PSALM 126:3 (NIV)

I have trouble parting with sentimental items. Even a greeting card scrawled with an illegible signature and no message finds its way into my keepsake drawer, which is already too full to close.

My sister suggested I pick up each item and ask myself, "Does this spark joy?" If not, I should discard it.

I placed the drawer on the bed. I decided I would make two piles—a "joy" pile on the left and a "no joy" pile on the right. Then I began.

Grandpa's small childhood Bible—joy pile. A nursery songbook I purchased with my tooth fairy money in 1965—joy pile. Grandchildren's artwork—joy pile. By the time I neared the bottom, it was clear that this drawer would never close. The last item was a simple white cardboard box.

I longed to play the piano as a child, but I was the youngest in my family of five, and most of the opportunities went to my older siblings. My older sisters took part in afterschool activities like the school band because my mother was available to drive them. When I reached third grade, Mom got a job. I became a latchkey kid who returned from school to an empty house, where I'd make myself a TV dinner. If I asked to learn to play the piano, I knew my parents would say it was too big and expensive, and who would take me to lessons? There was no point in asking.

I met my husband, Don, while I was in college. I'd had previous boyfriends, but nobody special. If I'd had the "spark joy" system back then, they would all be in the "no joy" pile. Don was different. He listened and seemed genuinely interested in what I had to say. He was a Christian, and, gradually, we began attending a local church. On our first visit, I was moved to tears as those around me worshipped God through music.

Before we got married, Don told me that he had prayed God would provide his future wife. Soon after he met me, he knew I was a gift from God—an answer to his prayer. I hadn't explicitly prayed for a spouse as Don did, but I knew that God had provided me with exactly who I needed.

One Christmas morning, he handed me a small, white box. Inside were tiny packages wrapped in white tissue, numbered 1 through 8. Don told me to unwrap them in numerical order.

The first package contained a tiny handmade couch. The second revealed a coffee table, the third an end table. Each item I unwrapped was a miniature replica of the furniture in our living room until I got to package number eight, which contained a teensy grand piano.

"That's your gift," Don said. "They were supposed to deliver it tomorrow morning, but with the blizzard, it won't arrive for at least a week."

I looked at him dumbly.

"The piano," he reiterated. "On our third date, you mentioned you wished you'd learned to play the piano, remember?"

I remembered. I couldn't believe Don did.

I glanced down at the items I'd unwrapped. "You made all of these?"

"Yep," he said. "The box lid represents our living room, and I built the furniture to scale. You can arrange it to decide where the piano should go."

When the piano arrived, I knew exactly where to place it, thanks to the little white box. It was a perfect fit.

I felt silly as an adult practicing "Mary Had a Little Lamb" at my instructor's house, but I enjoyed learning to play just as much as I imagined I would.

That was 37 years ago. We still have the piano. These days, it's a bit out of tune, and some keys stick; it would take some work to be usable again. But next year my husband and I are semi-retiring, and I plan to get it—and me!—tuned up and ready to play.

I put the white cardboard box in my joy pile. It will always remind me of God's bigger gift—bringing my husband and I together as one. My husband and I aren't perfect as individuals, but together we're a perfect fit.

—*Kristy Dewberry*

WHAT WILL YOU FIND?

Do you have a keepsake drawer or a place where you keep sentimental items? Set aside some time to go through it. Every time you come to an item that sparks joy, stop and remember how you got it and why it makes you happy. Then thank God for sending that joy your way.

In the Words on a Pendant

Your eyes saw my unformed body; all the days ordained for me were written in your book before one of them came to be.
—PSALM 139:16 (NIV)

Unwrapping the birthday package from my aunt, I gently pulled out a necklace. The words "Your story matters" were engraved on its silver pendant. As I held it, I thought back to the biggest chapters in my life story: many moves to new homes, marriage, and the birth of my three sons. But among them were moments that felt less significant, even moments I regretted. Did all of it truly matter? What can God make of the less-than-shiny interludes between celebrations or victories?

Holding the pendant then, I couldn't know then how much I would need those words just a year and a half later.

We had only known about our baby for two days when I miscarried. A raging current of emotions threatened to overtake me as I grappled with the hows and whys. In the days following, I scoured the internet for answers. I mostly found well-intentioned yet unhelpful results with statements like, "early miscarriages are common." But there is nothing normal about losing a child. I was convinced that this part of my story held some significance.

Fingering the necklace around my neck, I really looked at its words for the first time in a long time. *Your story matters.* I felt

God whispering the words to my heart as I read them. *Every part of your story matters.* This experience would bring some good into the world, even if I couldn't see how right now.

And it wasn't only my story that mattered. My little one's did, too, because their story would continue in glory, becoming more and more beautiful, and one day I would meet him or her and hear all about it.

The hardships and grief of life may try to overtake me. But when I touch my silver pendant, I'm reminded I have a redeeming and restoring God who only writes excellent stories, and who's not finished with mine yet.

—*Eryn Lynum*

WHAT WILL YOU FIND?

Find a necklace, pendant, decoration, or rock that has a word or phrase on it that reminds you of God's redeeming work in your life. Keep it with you, and pull it out whenever you need a reminder of the unique way God is working out your story.

In a Stack of Wooden Blocks

Be completely humble and gentle; be patient, bearing with one another in love. Make every effort to keep the unity of the Spirit through the bond of peace.
—EPHESIANS 4:2–3 (NIV)

My husband knew as soon as I arranged the six chunky wooden blocks on the sales counter that his wallet didn't stand a chance. I had rummaged for 20 minutes through a home store's barrel of scrap wood cutouts to find the perfect haul. Perspiring but splinter-free, I emerged from the barrel victorious. Each of the blocks I'd found had metal letters glued onto them. Together, they spelled our last name, D-A-V-I-E-S.

"Can we get them?" I asked.

It was a loaded question. Finances were tight, so the $10 per block price was stretching it. I was grateful our last name wasn't Westmoreland or Featherstonehough.

It had been a challenging season for our family, and the imperfectly cut wood blocks seemed like they were fashioned just for us. Maybe just *like* us. Different grains and sizes. Slightly disjointed and rough around the edges. And yet there were growth rings, too.

When I arranged them into sequence, it was like God whispered, "Look at how beautiful they are together."

We bought the blocks.

They have held a place of honor on my mantel for at least 10 years. God's whisper in that store really has been true across all that time. Individually, each block is different and a little dinged-up. I even dropped the letter A when dusting once, leaving an unfortunate dent in the corner. But by God's grace, the D-A-V-I-E-S—and the Davies—are still standing side-by-side.

And God was right. They are beautiful together.

—*Laurie Davies*

WHAT WILL YOU FIND?

Ask God to reveal the "growth rings" in your family members. Set aside time to call, text, or tell them you appreciate how much they have grown in character, humility, or courage. You've all been through a lot together. Today is a good day to applaud their growth!

In a Photo Album

Also at your times of rejoicing ... you are to sound the trumpets over your burnt offerings and fellowship offerings, and they will be a memorial for you before your God.
—NUMBERS 10:10 (NIV)

Approaching our twenty-fifth wedding anniversary, circumstances shouted the truth that my husband and I held decidedly different goals, desires, and dreams. Spinning our wheels with little common ground, we made no progress forward—and certainly none toward each other. I began to despair that our silver anniversary would prove simply a cold, gray symbol to mark the passage of time rather than a victorious accomplishment to celebrate.

God prompted me to go to work on a project, a surprise anniversary gift for my husband. Although my heart was not in it, I pressed forward, sorting through photo albums to create a PowerPoint slideshow that would highlight our history together. Little did I know what would happen in my own heart.

The pictures carried me back in time. High school graduation, followed shortly by our wedding. College graduation. Children. Various moves to new homes. As the years stretched out in front of my eyes, reminding me of hard times and happy times alike, I felt my heart softening. Somehow the issue at hand no longer remained the insurmountable monster it had been. *See?* I could sense God whispering. *What you have is too valuable to throw away.*

The slideshow was done by the day of our twenty-fifth anniversary. Set to Kenny Rogers' "Through the Years," I could see that it had as powerful an impact on my husband as it did on me. We both realized we did indeed have much to celebrate.

God established festivals of remembrance for His people because He knows how quickly we forget. Now, whenever I look at those old albums, I don't just remember the memories they represent—I remember the God who sat with me and reminded me what's worth holding on to.

—Terrie Todd

WHAT WILL YOU FIND?

Is there someone or something in your life you take for granted? Do you feel yourself falling into a nasty swamp of disenchantment? Find something that reminds you of your history with that person, and listen for what God whispers to you about the future.

Watching from Her Doorway

For all who are led by the Spirit of God are children of God. So you have not received a spirit that makes you fearful slaves. Instead, you received God's Spirit when he adopted you as his own children. Now we call him, "Abba, Father."
—ROMANS 8:14–15 (NLT)

I watched from her bedroom doorway as my 1-year-old foster daughter happily pulled every book off her bookshelf. The image clogged my throat with gratitude. We had just started the long process of her adoption, and with all my heart, I wanted her to know that she *belonged*. She was my daughter. This was *her* room. Those were *her* books. I wanted her to understand that she was free to enjoy all the rights and privileges that came with being a member of our family—including the right to make a mess. And here she was, comfortably doing just that.

Leaning against my daughter's doorframe, Romans 8 came to mind—reminding me that I, too, am an adopted child of God. Was I living confidently, secure in my family position? Did I understand that I don't have to be perfect? That, like my daughter, I have the right to make a mess?

God invites us to call Him *Daddy*, "Abba" (Romans 8:15). And we are promised an incredible future as fellow heirs with Christ (verse 17). Because we belong to God, we can enjoy all the rights and privileges as a member of His family.

It's easy for me to feel *tolerated* by God. Like I made it into His family by the skin of my teeth. But God doesn't want us tiptoeing around our relationship to Him any more than I want my daughter tiptoeing around her place in our family.

Standing in the doorway, I felt a renewed invitation to live confidently as God's daughter. And if I make a mess along the way, I know He's still proud of my effort towards growth.

—Kate Rietema

WHAT WILL YOU FIND?

Today, pray using the name *Abba,* Daddy. Take time to imagine yourself in a tender parent-child scene with God. Then ask God what He loves about you—listen and write it down. We are cherished children! Let's live like it!

At an Ordinary Table

For he chose us in him before the creation of the world to be holy and blameless in his sight. In love, he predestined us for adoption to sonship through Jesus Christ, in accordance with his pleasure and will—to the praise of his glorious grace, which he has freely given us in the One he loves.
—EPHESIANS 1:4-6 (NIV)

It was an ordinary booth in a typical family-style restaurant. I sat quietly on a worn, green vinyl bench on one side of the table. Across from me sat a husband and wife squeezed in side by side, Bill and Jean. Their eyes shone as if sharing an inside joke.

When the waiter visited our table, it was obvious they'd met him before. They seemed like good friends. The conversation suddenly came into focus when Bill said, "I'd like to introduce you to our daughter—the one we never had, but always prayed for."

His wife looked at me and beamed. The sparkle in her eyes touched a tender place in my heart. I had never heard anyone admit they'd prayed for me. Not even my parents. Especially not my parents.

Memories from my childhood flooded back. I came into the world not even 11 months after my older sister, an unexpected pregnancy that overwhelmed my parents. My biological father ignored what he couldn't manage. It was as if he believed if he didn't pay attention to me, I wasn't there. My mother struggled with mental illness at a time when such things were never discussed, let alone addressed. Her hidden pain robbed her of strength. She didn't have the energy to take care of two little children. Experiencing safety meant trying to make myself invisible. My home was already crowded with unmet needs.

When I was 16, my parents finally divorced. They were busy with new relationships, and I rarely saw them.

I had only known Bill and Jean for a few months. I had been the 19-year-old bride unpacking wedding gifts in a tiny $250-a-month rental house that already felt like home; they were our next-door neighbors, living in a peaceful house shaded by pecan trees. My new husband was focused on building a successful career, and more often than not I was alone at home. Bill and Jean were excited to have a young woman close by who had plenty of time to be social.

Bill took me with him to pick out the tile he was going to install in my kitchen backsplash. He wanted the tiny space to make me smile even before I poured my morning coffee. Jean invited me for supper most evenings when my husband was working late. She taught me how to follow the recipes she'd learned from her own mother.

And then, this. The family that I so desperately needed, publicly claiming me. Telling their friend how they'd prayed for me to come into their lives. That night, I experienced for the first time what it was like to be part of the family of God. God is proud of me, not hiding me. I am not invisible; I am celebrated. I am not a problem; I am planned for. I am not an orphan; I am a child of the King. I found God there, sitting in the green booth at a family restaurant.

Jesus joyfully offers us a seat at His table. We are adopted into His inheritance. We live out this good news in communion with Him. We get to say, "Yes!" when He invites us to "Taste and see that the LORD is good" (Psalm 34:8, NIV).

—*Janet Newberry*

WHAT WILL YOU FIND?

Take the time to sit at an ordinary table. Close your eyes and ask the Father to reveal that He's sitting with you. Notice the sparkle in His eyes. Then listen with your heart. What does the voice of Love say to you?

On a Mountain Trail

He made my feet like the feet of a deer and set me secure on the heights.
—PSALM 18:33 (ESV)

After a couple hours of hiking up a steep, snow-covered trail, my husband and I, along with our four children, were nearly at the mountain's summit. The trees thinned, exposing us to the vast expanse of the Rocky Mountains, and I noticed one of our sons growing nervous. We were completely safe, but his mind was beginning to convince him otherwise.

I could recognize the signs. Many times I had fallen under the same sudden anxiety on mountain trails, and I knew how to help. I placed my hand on his back, offering steady assurance. "Let's go a bit farther," I said, smiling at him. I fell into step at his right side, acting as a buffer between him and the downward-sloped hillside. Step by step, we continued toward the peak.

The trail narrowed around 100 feet before reaching the top, and he and I decided this was our stopping point. We knew our limits. But even so, it was a victory: this was a new limit, one we hadn't known we were capable of. My husband took our other children to the top while my son and I sat and took in the breathtaking expanse of surrounding summits. We might not have planted our feet at the top, but we made it much further than either of us thought we could.

As we descended the mountain, my son stayed by my side. "I'm going to come back here with my own kids someday," he told me. "And if they get scared, I'm going to help them find their new limits."

I felt God with both of us in those words—me next to my son, and Him next to both of us, holding our hands. So many times God has fallen into step beside me, gently encouraging me to go a bit farther as He steadies my stride, helping me press beyond limits and achieve more than I thought possible. And sometimes, when anxiety threatens to bring me to a halt, I can hear Him whisper, "Let's go a bit farther."

—*Eryn Lynum*

WHAT WILL YOU FIND?

Go on a walk or hike in nature and meditate on Psalm 18:33. Reflect on how God has helped you achieve your goals and taken you to new heights. Praise Him for His steadying hand as you pursue all He has for you.

In a Stack of Pennies

Whoever conceals their sins does not prosper, but the one who confesses and renounces them finds mercy.
—PROVERBS 28:13 (NIV)

As a preschooler, I received two pennies each Sunday to drop in the offering plate. It made me feel like part of the church family to make my own contribution, even though I'd done nothing to earn the money.

One Sunday, as the plate passed down the rows, it occurred to me the offering was optional. It also occurred to me that if I held back my pennies, I could buy myself a treat. I began to implement my plan, keeping the pennies in my little red purse. Each week, I stacked them higher on a shelf in my bedroom, no doubt rubbing my greedy little hands together and congratulating myself on my cleverness.

One night when Dad came to tuck me in, he noticed the growing stack. "Where did you get the pennies?"

"Um. I don't remember."

"Sounds like you're having a little memory trouble. Did you forget to put them in the offering?" Like he didn't already know.

Eventually, I 'fessed up. We talked about the plans I'd made for the money and Dad explained how it belonged to God and had come my way only by grace in the first place. I don't think he realized that in his gentle correction, he was showing me God. No punishment. No condemnation. Just like

Jesus with the woman caught in adultery, Dad's message was "go and sin no more." I knew I was loved, the same way that God loves all of us, even when we make bad choices.

To this day, I keep a small stack of pennies in view to remind me of the lesson Dad taught me that day. Genuine treasure comes in the form of mercy, love, and grace.

—*Terrie Todd*

WHAT WILL YOU FIND?

Think of a time you experienced God's forgiveness and mercy. Where were you? Was anyone with you? Do you have a reminder of that time that you still keep? If you don't have one, find or make one. Keep it somewhere that you can see it, as a touchstone for the times when you know you've made mistakes.

Eating Fried Chicken and Biscuits

Wisdom has built her house; she has set up its seven pillars. She has prepared her meat and mixed her wine; she has also set her table.
—PROVERBS 9:1-3 (NIV)

Platters of fried chicken, bowls of steaming vegetables, and a basket of homemade biscuits filled my Southern mother-in-law's table one summer afternoon. After the blessing, we pulled up our chairs to the table, filled our plates, and poured glasses of iced tea. Butter on the biscuits and a side of fresh cucumbers and tomatoes delighted our tastebuds.

Memories of that afternoon and many more gatherings just like it stayed with me through the years, coming back to me every time I ate particularly delicious fried chicken. It happened again recently when my husband I were dining at a family-style restaurant at a mountain inn. I remarked on how good his mother-in-law's food had been. "We never left her table hungry."

That day, the words struck a chord in me. There is someone else who prepares a table for me and never lets me leave hungry. Every morning I sit down at God's table when I focus on Him in prayer and Bible study, and I silently thank Him for the blessings He provides. He invites me to fill my plate with tailor-made blessings, scriptures, and opportunities to honor Him and serve others in Jesus's name.

God's food is even better than fried chicken: it's forgiveness when I sin, peace when I'm anxious, hope when I'm discouraged, wisdom when I face dilemmas. I can cry with sorrow or laugh with joy while I talk with Him and seek counsel in His Word. His gift is His presence, and just like a gathering at my mother-in-law's house, I know when I sit down at the table I will always leave full. I can taste His goodness every day, and it never fails to fill me with gratitude.

—*Jeannie Waters*

WHAT WILL YOU FIND?

Designate a place to meet God at His table daily.

Place your Bible, a journal, and a pen in a basket.

Before you read Scripture, ask God to teach you, meet your needs, and provide opportunities to honor Him by serving others and sharing your relationship with Jesus.

My Grandma's Class Ring

*Samuel then took a large stone and placed it between the towns of Mizpah and Jeshanah. He named it Ebenezer (which means "the stone of help"), for he said, "Up to this point the L*ORD *has helped us!"*
—1 SAMUEL 7:12 (NLT)

I often fiddle with my right ring finger, twirling the 1932 high-school class ring made for far daintier hands than mine. The ring belonged to my grandma, and in order to resize and wear it, I had to submit it to a skilled jeweler's fire and cutting process.

I'll never forget the day my grandma gave the ring to me. Reminiscing about my grandpa, my grandma answered the sorts of questions from me that the Greatest Generation usually doesn't entertain. *When did you kiss grandpa the first time? When did you know you were in love? What did you think was grandpa's cutest feature?*

They'd been married 65 years. We had buried him that afternoon.

Grandma excused herself to go upstairs. I followed. She was rummaging for something.

"I want you to have this," she said, her voice breaking as she placed her class ring into my hand. No further words were spoken. She was from stoic German stock, after all.

Though she never told me in so many words why she gave me her ring, I thought it might be her way of saying "thank you" for stirring memories from a season so very long ago. Or perhaps it was to offer me, even in her own grief, a tangible marker of how long my grandparents had loved—and *lived*.

She's with the Lord now. And like that 1932 class ring I wear on my finger, she had been through a fire and cutting process, too. Two world wars. A stillborn baby. Widowhood.

Grandma gave me more than a piece of jewelry that day. She gave me a symbol of longevity and endurance. And like Samuel placing an Ebenezer stone—a "stone of help"—in the ground, she passed on a tangible reminder that "up to this point, the Lord has helped us."

What's your reminder?

—*Laurie Davies*

WHAT WILL YOU FIND?

If you have an "Ebenezer stone"—a tangible keepsake that reminds you of how far God has brought you—wear it or place it where you can see it today. Consider how God has helped you in the past and declare your thanks, in faith, for His help in the future.

CHAPTER 8

finding God in ordinary moments

Wearing an Avon Calling Pin

"Here I am! I stand at the door and knock. If anyone hears my voice and opens the door, I will come in and eat with that person, and they with me."
—REVELATION 3:20 (NIV)

The gold Avon Calling door knocker pin that I'd tossed in the bottom of my junk drawer was a symbol of shame. It was no more real gold than I had a real future, of course. Disfigurement from facial tumors and seizures had rendered me an outcast at high school. A school administrator deemed that I wasn't a candidate for college. Or much of anything. They decided that I'd be less disruptive if they found me a job.

I ended up peddling cosmetics door-to-door. An Avon lady. Except I wasn't a lady, just a kid who didn't fit in anywhere. They gave me a zipped tweed satchel filled with samples of lipsticks and fragrances with names like *Unforgettable* and *Here's My Heart*. I'd be unforgettable all right. I wasn't so sure about the heart part.

My first day, I stepped onto a little porch and straightened the faux gold door knocker on the collar of my Peter Pan blouse. Stared at my first doorbell and raised a shaky finger to ring it. A lady peeked out from behind a curtain and shook her head.

Rejection—the story of my life.

Why did life have to be so hard? Seeking solace, I thought of Daddy's stories. I woke up to them, went to sleep hearing them. On weekends at the flea market with him, tales were as plentiful as the treasures that we sought among the tables of used goods for sale. I grew to see stories as treasures too. When life got hardest and took me to doctors' waiting rooms, stories eased my fears. Listening and sharing formed a bond of connection like no other.

The next house on the block was a sweet white cottage with a latticework trellis of climbing pink roses. It had a story feel. Suddenly, so did I. It was as if God was touching my shoulder, whispering in my ear. *Don't give up. Listen for the stories.*

I rang that second doorbell, determined to listen up if its door opened wide. When it did, I passed my little color brochure to the apron-clad lady of the house. Spritzed some *Here's My Heart* cologne from a tiny sky-blue bottle. "My mother's favorite fragrance," she declared, sniffing her wrist with a smile. Then told me about other things her mother loved. Like calico fabric and ribbons with polka dots and banana pudding with vanilla wafers. Told me that her mother would have loved me, too, if I'd appeared at her door. After years of rejection, suddenly I was wanted. Everything turned around in that one visit.

My passion for stories—hearing them and then writing them down—grew with every doorbell I rang. I filled spiral notebooks with the enchantment hidden behind closed doors. When someone turned me away, I'd just ring another doorbell, because the best story (and sale) might be waiting at the next house. The folks I met were what a kid with a serious illness craved. People with life experience, wisdom, and encouragement to pass on. With huge hearts. Folks who believed in dreams and coaxed me to do the same. Who assured me that I could be and do anything I set my mind to.

Their stories lit my soul and made me feel alive. I began to see a picture of my future—not as an outcast but as a helper, tending to those like me who hurt inside and out. I made up my mind to go back to school and become a nurse. But I so enjoyed being an Avon lady, I continued to ring doorbells until I finally graduated and embarked on that nursing career.

Life was to take me in many directions. What I learned in those welcoming places informed every step of my journey. Stories weren't simply my survival. I've told them as a professor, a mental health therapist, an author of textbooks, a researcher, a home decor stylist, a motivational speaker. Most cherished of all, as a writer for inspirational publications. My business card sums up my calling in a single sentence: "A story is the shortest distance between two hearts."

The God who told stories was onto something. Whether we're touting bubble bath, mending a fence with a neighbor, teaching a class, or putting our heart on paper, the fastest way to connect is with a story. The best day of my life was when I asked God to be the author of my story. The second-best day was when I discovered Avon Calling had not been a punishment but a divine detour. God's oh-so-personal provision.

Today my door-knocker pin isn't relegated to a junk drawer. I wear it proudly on a necklace of treasured charms. I doubt it would sell for more than a quarter, but to me it's solid gold—a reminder that God knew what my broken heart needed most. Avon Calling had shown me *my* calling.

—*Roberta Messner*

WHAT WILL YOU FIND?

As you walk through your world today, keep your eyes and ears open for the stories in your path. Ask God to help you see Him hidden in them, to bring His goodness out into the open through the sharing of them. To see the unique story God is writing with *your* life.

Writing in My Daily Journal

Come and hear, all you who fear God; let me tell you what he has done for me. I cried out to him with my mouth; his praise was on my tongue.... Praise be to God, who has not rejected my prayer or withheld his love from me!
—PSALM 66:16–17, 20 (NIV)

It is the end of the day, and I sit at my desk and do what I always do at day's end—I write in my journal. I have been keeping a daily journal for decades. I write about the events of the day, my feelings, my prayers, what I am thinking about. I know this sounds strange, but somehow I don't know what I think unless I write it on paper.

Today was not a good day, and I am not in a good mood. The dishwasher has developed a leak. My arthritic knee is acting up. The deer and the raccoons take turns trashing my garden. My neighbor sawed down a dead ash tree, and it fell across my fence, smashing the railings to toothpicks. "Sorry," he says meekly, and I know he means it, but I am not happy. To top it all off, my Detroit Tigers lost yet again; already fifteen games out of first place, and it's only June. Not a good day.

I begin to write. But then, abruptly, I stop. I can feel the spirit of God moving in me, reminding me of how blessed I am, and how foolish it is to focus only on the negative. "Sorry," I say meekly, and I mean it. I cross out what I have written and begin anew: "I am alive. I have a wonderful wife and a wonderful life. My children have grown to be fine, upstanding adults, and my grandchildren run to my arms even when my hands are empty. I am God's beloved child, and I am on the road to heaven."

It's been a good day.

—*Louis Lotz*

WHAT WILL YOU FIND?

Do you keep a daily journal? If not, try starting one. Write your reflections on paper, or on the computer. How have you felt the movement of God's spirit in your life lately? What do you sense God is calling you to do, and what would your life look like if you gave yourself permission to do that?

In the Sunlight on the Ocean

In the same way, let your light shine before others, that they may see your good deeds and glorify your Father in heaven.
—MATTHEW 5:16 (NIV)

I was captivated. The beauty unfolding before me engaged every sense—the sound of the gentle lapping of waves upon the shore, the feel of the sand between my toes, the smell of the ocean air, the salty taste of ocean on my lips. And there in front of me, the bright glow of the setting sun.

I'd been to the ocean many times, but this moment was different. What most caught my eye was the sparkling pathway of sunlight reflecting off the ocean surface. Like a glittering roadway, it drew my eyes directly to the magnificence of the setting sun.

I felt a nudge in my heart. *That's you. Those are my people.* A smile spread across my face. *Yes!* We are each like one of those crested waves when we love Jesus, when we sit in His presence, when we do the good works He has set in place of us to do. Light shines from us. We reflect His goodness. We glitter with His love. And anyone on the shore who sees us all doing what we were created to do can follow the path of reflected light directly to the Son. We are that brilliant pathway, that bright and beautiful road, drawing people's eyes to our glorious Savior.

—Elsa Kok Colopy

WHAT WILL YOU FIND?

Go to a nearby body of water—the largest one you can find—at sunset. Watch how the sun is reflected in the water, and open yourself to God's presence. How does He shine through you as you ebb and flow and live and love?

In the Desert, Under the Stars

The desert and the parched land will be glad; the wilderness will rejoice and blossom. Like the crocus, it will burst into bloom; it will rejoice greatly and shout for joy.
—ISAIAH 35:1–2 (NIV)

The Negev Desert sprawls, empty, lifeless. When the sun finally drops, it does so with reluctance, apparently too tired to continue inflicting damage. Darkness closes quickly out here, unapologetic and complete. I'm alone on this road. I hit the gas, liking the speed as I press into the night.

Sometime later I feel the need to stretch. My tires crunch gravel as I pull to the shoulder. I kill the ignition and turn off the headlights, step out of the car and breathe in the desert, enjoying the warm, paper-dry air after the air-conditioned chill. A quick stop is all I intend, but the silence holds me, a minute, then two. I find myself walking out into the desert. Behind me, the engine ticks as it cools. My eyes adjust and I pause. I hold up my arms and hands. I am literally bathed in starlight.

My eyes are pulled skyward. I turn a slow circle, dazed by the heavenly riot above me. I've never seen so many stars. Horizon to horizon they fill the sky. Shimmering, dancing. So bright and intense I can practically hear their vibration.

I am in awe. What kind of God could imagine a sky like this? Fill it to overflowing with moons and suns and planets and . . .

A breeze rises, pulling me back to earth. I shiver, though I am not cold. I am not here by accident. I have been called to this place. *Empty and lifeless*? I couldn't have been more wrong.

This desert, this *moment,* isn't lifeless at all. It is filled to the brim with *being*. With essence and soul. Filled with God and His radical, star-drenched love.

It's so easy to get wrapped up in my own little world, to forget I am only a microscopic part of an immense reality. I thank God for His timely reminders.

—*Buck Storm*

WHAT WILL YOU FIND?

Have you ever been in a place where you could bathe in starlight? A desert, a mountaintop, an open field with the wide sky above? The next time you feel God calling you to a place like that, follow His nudge, and see the wonders He shows you.

In the Dairy Aisle

Do not forget to do good and to share with others, for with such sacrifices God is pleased.
—HEBREWS 13:16 (NIV)

The usual frenzy thrummed through the grocery store. Heads down, lists clutched, everyone hustled by, strangers in a silent ballet. But last week, something snagged my attention as I neared the dairy coolers. A frail hand, etched with a map of blue veins, strained to reach the top shelf. An elderly woman struggled to lift a gallon of milk she couldn't quite manage. Suddenly, a lanky teen, earbuds dangling, showed up beside her. With a basketball player's grace, he snagged the milk, then placed it gently in her basket.

Her eyes crinkled in gratitude. "Thank you, young man," she rasped, her voice thick with emotion, as she reached into her pocket for a crumpled dollar bill. She offered it to the boy, but he flashed a grin, the kind that reached his eyes, and shook his head.

"We all need a little help sometimes," he said, his words genuine. He took her small hand in his strong one and gave it a gentle squeeze.

Warmth spread through me as I witnessed this exchange. I saw God at work in that simple act of reaching for a carton of milk. The teenage boy didn't hesitate to help; his kindness and selflessness reflected God's caring. The woman's gratitude, even without words, expressed the ripple effect of such a small gesture. In that crowded aisle, amid the hustle and bustle, God reminded me of the power of compassion and the importance of seeing the divine in the everyday acts of those around us.

—Elly Gilbert

WHAT WILL YOU FIND?

God's love can appear in the world in any place, at any time—and you can be an example of that love yourself. The next time you go to the grocery store, or other place with a lot of people, be alert for people you might be able to help in little ways. Ask God to lead you in finding opportunities to show His love to others.

In an Old Joke

Can a man hide himself in secret places so that I cannot see him? declares the LORD. Do I not fill heaven and earth?
—JEREMIAH 23:24 (ESV)

Harold was still substitute teaching at the age of 85. He spent most of his adult life as a missionary, teaching Sunday school to children in Tokyo, where only 2 percent of the population are Christian. Harold loved children, and he loved Jesus.

When Harold retired to the United States, he and his wife were members of the same church I attended, and I was blessed to get to know them well. I loved and respected this couple very much.

My children would return home with funny stories when Harold would sub in their classrooms. When explaining to students where Japan is, he was known to use one of the children's heads as a globe. He would place his finger on the child's forehead and tell them, "This is where we are now." He would then move his finger and poke the child in the back of the head saying, "Oops. Rough landing." He told us he used the same joke when explaining to Japanese children how far away the USA is.

When I learned that I would spend two weeks in Japan, I was excited to tell Harold. I asked him to help me select a gift for the host family I would stay with. Together, we chose an English/Japanese Bible.

During my first week in Japan, I toured Kyoto with my travel group. We saw several Shinto shrines and Buddhist temples, but no churches at all. Later in the day, I noticed a huge billboard on the top of a building that displayed a picture of Jesus. I asked if this was a Christian church. Our guide quickly set me straight. "No," he said. "Pachinko." Although gambling is illegal in Japan, legal loopholes have allowed for pachinko to be the exception.

I asked the obvious question. "Why is Jesus on the pachinko building?"

"Ah," he said. "Jesus is good luck!"

I began to wonder how my gift of a Bible would be received. I didn't sense any animosity toward Christianity from the Japanese people I met, but rather skepticism. Jesus was a good luck charm portrayed in a cartoonish way.

I whispered a brief prayer. "Lord, I don't see evidence of Jesus in Japan, but I know You are near."

My hosts for the second week were a couple in their mid-sixties. The language barrier was profound. When I was introduced to my host father, he held up two fingers and said, "English: Okie dokie, and oh my God." These were the only English phrases he understood. It was two phrases more than my host mother knew, and my Japanese was very limited. We communicated primarily through drawing, charades, and a lot of laughter. I was amazed at how we were able to bond with one another without words. I loved them.

On my final night in Japan, my host parents invited a young woman to join us for dinner who could interpret our conversation. During this dinner, they tested my new chopstick skills by having me pick up one fish egg and one grain of rice at a time. I shared pictures of my home in Michigan, and we talked about our families. It was during this meal that I chose to give the wrapped Bible to my new friends, explaining that this represented an important part of my life and that I wanted to wish them love and peace.

My host father, who was typically animated and gregarious, became very quiet. Was he offended by the gift? I then gave them oven mitts shaped like the state of Michigan and showed them where my hometown was on the mitten. The interpreter thought this was funny and asked, "Where is Michigan?"

In honor of Harold, I put my finger on the young woman's forehead and said, "This is where we are now . . ."

As I poked her in the back of the head, my host father said in clear English, "Oops. Rough landing."

As our eyes met, I could see tears in his eyes. He spoke to our young interpreter, and she relayed his message.

"Your host father attended Sunday school in Tokyo as a child. You have brought back special memories."

Harold had taught my host father in Tokyo 50 years earlier! I felt Jesus next to me then, whispering that He was not only in Japan, but in the hearts of believers everywhere.

—*Lisa Saruga*

WHAT WILL YOU FIND?

Did one of your teachers have a favorite joke that all of their students knew? Share it with someone today, either someone who knew that particular person or a member of a younger generation. Watch the way that jokes can spread and connect us together.

While Restoring the Floor

Therefore, if anyone is in Christ, the new creation has come: The old has gone, the new is here!
—2 CORINTHIANS 5:17 (NIV)

My back ached from days of bending over while installing flooring. This was *not* my area of expertise. But when my husband and I had the opportunity to buy my childhood home from my parents, we couldn't turn it down, even though the house would need a lot of work. It had been two weeks since we moved into the house with our four children to focus on the restoration. It was one of the biggest challenges I'd ever faced, and I felt my resolve waning each day.

Then one afternoon I glanced over to see my four-year-old daughter playing with her toys on a section of still-unfinished floor space. Immediately, my mind traveled back nearly three decades to myself at her age, playing with toys in the same spot, with my parents restoring these very floors.

I suddenly felt as if I was there with them, feeling their aching backs reflected in my own. They had done so much to make a home for me and my siblings. How many times had I run and slid across the wooden floorboards in games of chase? How many times had I swept them clean over the years? Two weeks before, when we arrived to begin work, the worn floorboards told stories of my childhood. And now, God had given me the gift of bringing life full circle.

As we worked side-by-side with our kids, God gave me another opportunity: He revealed to me the significance of restoration. Restoring a house was hard, but how much weightier and painful was the work God went through to restore my heart and make it new by sacrificing His Son on the cross?

As I knelt over the floorboards in the days that followed, my back still hurt, but my resolve never wavered again. God was with me the whole time, showing me that restoration is beautiful work.

—*Eryn Lynum*

WHAT WILL YOU FIND?

Choose something old to make new. It could be a chipped vase, a worn blanket, or an old, framed photo. Select something that holds a memory and restore it in a way that brings that memory to life again.

Sailing Next to a Whale

Some went down to the sea in ships... they saw the deeds of the LORD, his wondrous works in the deep.
—PSALM 107:23-24 (ESV)

Oh God, Thy sea is so great and my boat is so small... I kept the old Breton fisherman's prayer mounted on the bulkhead of my 24-foot sailboat.

Out on the open ocean, the sentiment really hit. Blue blanket of sky stretched huge. A thousand feet of darker blue water beneath. A couple of humpback whales spouted a hundred yards away and I felt my already insignificant vessel shrink a couple feet.

No phones, no life distractions, just me, my boat, and Him.

"Oh God, Thy sea is so great..."

I didn't expect an answer, of course. But if there's one thing I've found to be true through the years, it's that God is the master of the unexpected. His reply came in the form of another spout, much closer this time. Another whale arching to dive. I watched and waited for the fluke. A second or two later a stunning realization set in—this was not a humpback. I was witnessing an incredibly rare sight, a blue whale, the largest mammal on the planet, just off my beam. I held my breath as nearly 100 feet of magnificent animal arched through the water. I shouted out loud when the massive fluke rose, the spray throwing a dozen rainbows through the sunlight.

I believe in my heart God loves to surprise and delight us with even the smallest things. Sometimes He throws in a massive gift as well.

Yes, my boat was small. Even so He held it, and me, in his grip.

—*Buck Storm*

WHAT WILL YOU FIND?

God is constantly showing Himself. I believe He delights in it. When you go out today—wherever life happens to take you—keep your eyes open. Is God showing you something small? Something big? Something rare? Or is He in some everyday item whose meaning only the two of you know?

Wearing a Nun's Habit

When Peter saw him, he asked, "Lord, what about him?" Jesus answered, "If I want him to remain alive until I return, what is that to you? You must follow me."
—JOHN 21:21-22 (NIV)

Have you ever watched a movie and noticed that nuns tend to swivel the entire upper half of their bodies whenever they need to look to one side? I discovered the reason for this when I was cast as one of the nuns in *The Sound of Music* in a local community theater production. The coif, a sort of cap that covers the cheeks and neck, combined with a veil, works in the same way as horse blinders. Whether or not this was the original intent of the garments' design, the person wearing them is forced to either perform this turning maneuver or remain focused on whatever lies straight ahead.

In a horse, blinders work to keep them calm as they trust their driver with distractions that could derail them. It's not hard to see the application for humans. As I wore the nun's habit throughout the production, the action of turning my head became a reminder of God's presence: *Don't worry so much about the distractions. Keep your eyes straight ahead, and trust Me.*

To this day, whenever I see a nun's habit, I'm reminded to mind my own business. When I take my focus off God and His plan for me, it's much too easy to become jealous, resentful, and bitter. I wonder why God grants someone else something I think He should grant me as well. Or I can become immersed in life's many distractions, veering off the path my loving Father set for me. But when I put my spiritual blinders on, I'm reminded to live a life of obedience, devotion, and faith.

—*Terrie Todd*

WHAT WILL YOU FIND?

Try spending a few hours in a garment that restricts your peripheral vision and forces you to look straight ahead. Take note of your observations. Is God speaking to you through the experience? What can you gain from it? How might it help you remember to trust Him?

In a Crossword Puzzle

*A word fitly spoken is like apples
of gold in a setting of silver.*
—PROVERBS 25:11 (ESV)

My mom tossed her mechanical pencil on the coffee table. "I give up. I can't finish this crossword puzzle. I need a word for a narrow space between two mountains."

"What about *gorge*?" I asked.

"The word has six spaces."

I tried again. "Maybe *valley*?"

She shook her head. "No, there's already an *n* in the fifth position."

"Canyon fits the description, but the *n* wouldn't fall into the right place," I said. "Does *ravine* fit?"

She quickly grabbed her pencil, wrote the letters, and held up the puzzle. "That's it! Thanks. *Ravine* fits the clue and the number of spaces."

An ordinary, everyday exchange. But something about it stuck in my brain—a sense that I'd been missing something. The next day, glancing at the crossword puzzle book on the coffee table, it clicked into place: when doing a crossword, each word has to match the situation, both the clue and the designated number of spaces. You have to have both to make it fit.

That thought led to the memory of words I had spoken earlier that day: in haste and without a loving tone. They didn't fit the conversation well, and they may have hurt the other person.

God spoke to my heart, reminding me of Proverbs 25:11, and how my words should be chosen thoughtfully and spoken in love, "like apples of gold in a setting of silver." I asked Him to forgive me and help me to speak in ways that encourage others and offer grace, expressing the love of Christ. Now crossword puzzles will always remind me to make sure my words fit the situation—and not to give up if I can't find the right word right away.

—Jeannie Waters

WHAT WILL YOU FIND?

Use a website or concordance to find verses about the biblical use of words and speaking well. Write or print them. Place them in a prominent place and read one a day as a reminder to choose encouraging words that honor Christ. Ask God to help you speak words of beauty to others.

In the Autumn Leaves

"Is not wisdom found among the aged?
Does not long life bring understanding?
To God belong wisdom and power;
counsel and understanding are his."
—JOB 12:12–13 (NIV)

I understand that 40 is the new 20, and 50 is the new 30, but nobody has told my body that. Wrinkles are creeping in around the corners of my eyes, my neck isn't quite as taut and lovely as it once was, and various joints creek and pop like an out-of-tune folk band.

One quiet morning in our home in Colorado, I was lamenting the aging process. Out on the deck, the sun shone and warmed my face. It was a glorious fall morning, not too hot, not too cold. I looked out over our back yard and a bright shimmer drew my eye—the beautiful aspen in the southwest corner of our property. The deep green of the summer months had transitioned to a brilliant yellow as the weather cooled. Soon those brilliant leaves would fall to the ground, and in the spring new birth would come again. I marveled at how the sun captured the vibrant golden leaves. *Interesting,* I thought to myself, *how the leaves are most beautiful near the end of their life.*

Yes. It hit me. God nudged my aging heart. I too, am the most beautiful as I enter into my aging years. While I see wrinkles and hear popping, God sees brilliant beauty and perceives grace-filled wisdom. I am not fading as I draw closer to going home. I am only becoming more enchanting as I reflect my loving God to the world around me.

—*Elsa Kok Colopy*

WHAT WILL YOU FIND?

Do you live in an area of the country with changing leaves? Even if you don't, when fall comes, try to set aside some time to go out in nature while the leaves are changing. What are they whispering to you about the changing seasons in your own life? What parts of your past are bringing out your most beautiful colors today?

On an Empty Road

One thing I ask from the LORD, this only do I seek: that I may dwell in the house of the LORD all the days of my life, to gaze on the beauty of the LORD and to seek him in his temple.
—PSALM 27:4 (NIV)

It was an ordinary day. I had errands to run in a nearby town, and since the weather was clear and warm, I decided to take the back roads, enjoying the beautiful scenery along the way. I hopped into my Jeep and set out.

Driving past one farm after another, I slowed to take in the scent of meadowfoam blossoms, clover fields, and meadows awash in wildflowers. Passing a sheep ranch, I smiled. The Great Pyrenees dogs guarding the herd seemed a bit lazier than usual. Like them, I was in no hurry to get things done.

All at once, things changed. Time stood still. Everything became clearer to me, from the surrounding fields to the abundant life I have been blessed with. At that moment of heightened awareness, I sensed a presence in the car with me. God filled the interior space, delivering an almost palpable sensation of peace. It was as if I were wrapped in gentle arms, and a cloak of His love covered me. I wished the feeling of connectedness could stay with me forever, and struggled to hang on to the sacred sensation, but it slowly slipped away, as gentle as a caress.

God is with me always. But in my car that day—though I could never explain the whys or hows of that moment—I was blessed by a deep and personal communion with the Creator. I found God on an empty road, and I knew in that moment that with Him at my side, the future is as wide-open as the road ahead.

—Heidi Gaul

WHAT WILL YOU FIND?

Take a drive in the country. As you travel the back roads, clear your mind to focus on just one thought—God's constant presence in your life. Notice His fingerprints in your surroundings. Pray for heightened awareness of His being within, around, and with you.

Beneath the Weeping Willow

"Then he took some of the seed of the land and planted it in a fertile field; He placed it by abundant waters and set it like a willow tree."
—EZEKIEL 17:5 (NKJV)

Of all the trees in my grandparents' big backyard, the weeping willow was my favorite. It was one of the first trees to leaf out in spring and among the last to shed its leaves in fall. Its graceful, drooping branches reached all the way to the ground, creating the feeling of a private space underneath them. As a child, I loved to take a quilt from my grandmother's cedar chest and spread it on the ground beneath that willow. Sometimes I would lie there in the quiet and daydream. Sometimes I took an accidental nap. But most of the time, I read.

My favorite book? *The Bible Story* (volume one) by Arthur S. Maxwell, first published in 1953. I loved it not just because of its wonderful illustrations, but because it told about God in a way I could understand. I felt close to Him as I read the story of Creation, about Noah and the Tower of Babel and Abraham and Sarah and Isaac. In those stories, I learned about God's power and love.

My grandparents passed on to their heavenly reward many years ago. I still have one of Grandmother's quilts. I still have access to a wonderful weeping willow tree. But my battered copy of *The Bible Story* had gone missing. So, not long ago, inspired by seeing a copy in my dentist's waiting room, I ordered another.

The day it arrived, I gathered the quilt and the beloved blue book into my arms and slipped behind the quiet curtain of the willow tree. And—just as I had more than 60 years before—I found God in its pages. The colorful illustrations and the simple retellings of those dear old stories brought back the joy of a simple retelling of classic truths, and the wonder of feeling His presence next to me as I read.

—*Jennie Ivey*

WHAT WILL YOU FIND?

Do you have a favorite telling of stories from the Bible, one that especially speaks to your heart? Take a copy off your shelf—or find one if you don't still have a copy—and read it again. Relive all the ways that those stories lift you up and connect you with the Source of all life.

CHAPTER 9

finding God in the home

Sitting in a Wing Chair

I want you woven into a tapestry of love, in touch with everything there is to know of God.
—COLOSSIANS 2:2 (MSG)

While my sister underwent a medical procedure, I wandered into a nearby consignment shop. From the jewelry section, I heard a frail, male voice. "I thought you'd ask more than this!" The hush of sorrow was in those words. I leaned in for his story.

"There's not much call for dining room furniture," the proprietor explained. "Folks have turned their dining rooms into offices. Libraries. Passthroughs. The young kids don't cook much, you know. When they order takeout, they use paper plates."

I turned to see a white-haired gentleman holding onto a lovely antique walnut dining room table for dear life, shaking his head at the price tag. It must have been his own dining set, placed in this consignment shop in the hopes of that he would get some money when it sold. The nurse in me couldn't stand his pain. I edged over to try to console him. "I'm so sorry, sir," I began.

"We loved this set so," the man said. "Do you know how empty a room is without a dining room suite?" He was near tears now, staring at the matching buffet, his face bereft. Thanksgivings and Christmases and birthdays were reflected in his eyes as he met mine. His hands caressed the dining set's chairs. "I upholstered them myself," he said, voice thick with nostalgia. "That's real fine cloth."

My eyes caught sight of the fabric. It couldn't be. But it was—the identical geometric green fabric I'd used for a pair of wing chairs in my log cabin. A shiver went down my spine as I remembered. There had been 20 yards left on the bolt—a wonderful Robert Allen design—but I'd only needed 10. The store manager was adamant. He would not divide it. With a no-more-questions voice, he'd turned on his heels to get back to business.

I reached for the gentleman's thin hand. "You have excellent taste. Want to know how I know?" He nodded, mystified, as I pulled up a photo on my phone. Tapped it for a close-up view and told him the story of that mysterious afternoon that I'd gotten a call from the manager's office to come in, because the fabric was now available. The sales clerk who met me there was completely baffled. "It's the oddest thing. He just told me to split the yardage. Said it needs to go to two different homes. Some sort of a nudge he couldn't explain."

The mystery of that afternoon—the warp and woof of threads woven into fabric, into our lives—came together in a single moment. I stroked the green geometric print on the seat of one of the gentleman's six chairs and told him how that very fabric that had brought me so much pleasure on the two skirted wing chairs by my fireplace. They were vintage chairs, tall, straight out of a storybook. I'd found them when a daycare center called The Three Bears was closing. In my century-old cabin, they were fairy-tale perfect.

I grabbed a few pillows to show him how our green, goes-with-everything fabric would be perfect with florals and stripes, whatever a new home might have. "Your dining room set will find the right home, just like my chairs did," I reassured him. "God saved that fabric for something special."

I live by myself, with no one usually occupying my second wing chair. But when I sit across from it, I imagine God there. I ask Him to be with folks whose lives have changed. Who find themselves seemingly alone, like the gentleman in the thrift store. In my heart I still see his smile when he realized who had purchased the other 10 yards of his special cloth at Fabric World a decade before. Two strangers cut from the same cloth. Connected by far more than fabric in a story that's shaped by God.

—Roberta Messner

WHAT WILL YOU FIND?

Is there a story being told in the everyday of *your* life? At the local farm stand? The diner where you drink your morning brew? The place where you fill your car's tank? Listen in for God's presence in those not-so-ordinary moments. You may find yourself connected by more than strawberries and coffee.

On Go-Home Day

"I carried you on eagles' wings and brought you to myself."
—EXODUS 19:4 (NIV)

As a flight attendant, the best day of a trip is the day we get to fly home. The crew greets each other that last morning with the joy of announcing, "It's go-home day!"

And I'll let you in on a little secret. If you're aboard the final flight of that day, you're going to arrive early because the pilots are flying fast. We all just want to get home.

I was working one of these trips when I found out through social media that a dear friend had died of breast cancer. It had come on suddenly, and she hadn't had much time to fight it. She didn't live close by, so I'd sent her a bracelet in the mail and prayed. The unexpected loss shocked me and left me heartbroken for her devoted husband as well as our whole community.

In a daze, I read the pre-taxi announcements and performed my safety checks, then strapped into my jump seat for takeoff. As the plane sped down the runway to liftoff, the realization hit.

My friend had gone to be with the Lord. Today was her "go-home" day, too.

The rest of us were left behind and had every reason to mourn our pain, but it helped to think of my friend already there, finishing her last flight home to be with Jesus.

Outside the window, the wing of the airplane cut through the clouds into a brilliant blue sky, high up, where the sunshine can't be hidden. The hymn "I'll Fly Away" played through my head as I imagined my friend's arrival at her forever home.

In that moment, in the bittersweet excitement of the go-home day my friend and I shared, God made the hope of heaven real to me.

—Angela Ruth Strong

WHAT WILL YOU FIND?

Do you ever find yourself traveling far from home? Think of the feeling when you walk through your front door, returning to your place of safety and happiness. What must it be like to come home to heaven?

By a Front Door

He shielded him and cared for him; he guarded him as the apple of his eye, like an eagle that stirs up its nest and hovers over its young, that spreads its wings to catch them and carries them aloft.
—DEUTERONOMY 32:10-11 (NIV)

A few weeks ago, I was visiting family in my hometown. As I approached my childhood home, I could see the new exterior door that was recently installed on the front of the house. I'd seen the new door on a previous visit, but I still wasn't used to it. The old front door had been on my house for more than 40 years, and it represented more to me than just a metal structure.

During my high-school years, my dad watched me from that old front door to ensure I made it safely to the bus stop, which was several blocks down the street. Usually, my walks were uneventful. One morning, however, a car passed by me, and then I noticed it turn around and pass me again. I was well trained by my homicide detective dad; when the car made a right turn a block ahead of me and then slowed, I was worried about the driver's intentions. Fortunately, a neighbor was walking behind me. He didn't notice the car, but when I asked for help, he agreed to walk me to the bus stop. Seeing I was no longer alone, the suspicious car immediately took off.

A few seconds later, my dad pulled up to the bus stop. While watching me from the door, he had also noticed the suspicious vehicle pass by and wanted to ensure for himself that I was safe. That front door came to represent my father to me, and the safety and security of our home.

I grew up in an urban neighborhood that some might consider dangerous, but in spite of that, I knew I could always feel safe. No matter where I go, God knows exactly where I am at any moment. Like my earthly father, I know He will watch over me to keep me out of harm's way. And whether it's the old door or a new one, seeing the entrance to my childhood home reminds me that God's constant protection follows me wherever I go.

—*Ericka Loynes*

WHAT WILL YOU FIND?

Pick a door in your home. Go to it and intentionally open it. As you do, think about a door God has opened for you. How has He blessed your life through that opportunity? When you're ready—either in that moment or later—intentionally close a door in your home. Think about a door God has kept shut for you. How has His love and concern protected you?

Comforting My Anxious Goldendoodle

Don't be afraid. I am with you. Don't tremble with fear. I am your God. I will make you strong, as I protect you with my arm and give you victories.
—ISAIAH 41:10 (CEV)

The search was on for a hypoallergenic puppy—hypoallergenic because of my allergies and a puppy because they're cute and I'm crazy. But God had other plans. Our quest ended with a call from a friend asking if we would consider adopting a four-year-old goldendoodle.

We drove to the friend's house to meet Henry the Doodle. While we fell in love with his friendly disposition, my friend advised us to seriously consider his anxiety issues. I didn't know what "anxious" entailed, so I waved it off, figuring if anyone knew how to handle anxiety, it was me.

I had struggled with situational anxiety after a car accident. Initially limited to the highway where the accident occurred, fear had now crept into my everyday life, leaving me rattled and physically shaken every time I drove a long distance. *If I can learn to live with that*, I thought, *how bad can an anxious dog be?*

At first, Henry's anxiety was apparent only when left alone, but one day, while napping beside me, I noticed his jerking limbs and caught the sound of gnarly grinding coming from his mouth. I stretched out my arm, spread out my hand, and gently placed it on his head. "You're OK," I assured him quietly. "I'm here, and I won't leave you." His body instantly quieted to perfect stillness.

And in that moment, I sensed God beside me, whispering in my ear. *I'm here for you. Trust Me like Henry trusts you and be at peace.*

Soon after, an opportunity to travel to Tennessee arose. It involved driving on a stretch of windy roads I had avoided for years, but this time, remembering Henry and God's assurance of His presence, I said yes. Today, when I comfort Henry, I recall how God brought me full circle, and I whisper a prayer of gratitude into His ear.

—Cathy Baker

WHAT WILL YOU FIND?

Are there places or situations that make you anxious? The next time you're brought there, by choice or circumstance, close your eyes and open yourself to trust. Imagine God's hand on you and listen for His voice in your heart.

Holding a Treasured Coffee Mug

Your testimonies also are my delight and my counselors.
—PSALM 119:24 (NKJV)

Gazing at the chipped coffee mug on my desk, a wave of warm memories washes over me. The speckled ceramic cup with a stick-figure owl drawn on the front now sports a jagged chip on its rim—a scar from a late-night cram session gone wrong. But the imperfection only adds to its charm, a reminder of countless late-night conversations fueled by strong coffee and even stronger advice.

The mug was a gift from my beloved professor and mentor, Mary Jo. As I cradle it in my hands, I can almost hear Mary Jo's calm, reassuring voice guiding me through yet another challenge in my young life.

The bitter tang of cold coffee on my tongue brings back the memory of wrestling with a difficult decision about my major. Fear and uncertainty swirled in my head as I poured out my heart to Mary Jo in her tiny, book-lined office. The comforting aroma of freshly brewed coffee filled the air as she listened patiently, her gentle eyes reflecting my inner turmoil. Her insightful questions, challenging me to consider my strengths and passions, slowly chipped away at the fog of confusion.

In those moments, huddled over steaming mugs, a sense of calm settled over me. Mary Jo, my mentor, was a representation of God's unwavering belief in my potential. She didn't just throw me into the deep end. She was a wise and caring guide by my side. Her patience, her wisdom, and her steady support reflected God's character, a God who is both a guide and a source of encouragement—then and, as my chipped mug reminds me, always.

—*Elly Gilbert*

WHAT WILL YOU FIND?

As you reflect on your own journey, consider finding someone in your community who could benefit from your mentorship. Be a listener and a thought partner for them. Encourage them to follow God's guidance and demonstrate your confidence in their abilities.

On an Old Staircase

Make a joyful noise to the LORD, all the earth! Serve the LORD with gladness! Come into his presence with singing! Know that the LORD, he is God! It is he who made us, and we are his; we are his people, and the sheep of his pasture.
—PSALM 100:1–3 (ESV)

My home is a lovely 1912 farmhouse, complete with a laundry chute and a porch sporting a couple of rockers. But one of my favorite parts of the house is the staircase. It's nothing fancy—no sweeping curves or carved banisters. In fact, the stairs are quite steep and narrow, reminiscent of a ladder.

Why do I adore this feature of my house? It's one part of the structure that speaks. When the humidity causes its brittle, stiff boards to creak, I commiserate. But more often, those squeaks echo with the sound of rejoicing. Like me, those treads are making a joyful noise to the Lord. And there is plenty to celebrate. After all, every step I ascend brings me that much closer to heaven.

As I climb these steps, I pause to reflect on the many people who have gone up this staircase. I see the simple beauty and grace of life as years go by. God's presence filled this element of my home when it was mere lumber, and before that, when it was no more than a bunch of saplings in a dark forest. And every step—pardon the pun—of the way, is part of His sacred design. Just as my old staircase brings me joy, from my youth to gray hair to the promise of eternity, God delights in me. And I delight in the words of encouragement He shares through a creaky step.

—*Heidi Gaul*

WHAT WILL YOU FIND?

Find an old, creaky staircase, whether it's in your home, a friend's house, or a public building. Sit on a step, close your eyes, and listen... God is whispering that He loves you more, despite—and because—of your creaks. Like the staircase, you're beautiful as you stretch skyward, reaching for Him.

In a Spacious Place

*He brought me out into a spacious place;
he rescued me because he delighted in me.*
—PSALM 18:19 (NIV)

I'm envious, and oddly intimidated, by those who willingly and frequently open their homes to friends or even strangers who are passing through the area. "They must be extroverts," I tell myself.

I'm also happy to open my home—*after* I've had ample time to plan extra meals and restock extra migraine medication. I don't long for perfection, but for a simple, hospitable ease that welcomes guests to our home, even at a moment's notice.

Unwinding a resistance to new people in my home, so tightly wound over decades, is no easy feat. Still, a growing ache in my spirit nudges me to release self-imposed expectations, allowing space for others—and for Jesus to step into that space.

When we moved to a home swallowed up by four open acres and few trees, it didn't feel like home to me. I was a city girl from the South who grew up with trees crowded so close among the buildings that their branches hugged whole houses. But our new church became more like family, and my husband and I gladly offered to host our weekly small group.

The house was prepared. I was not. But laughter from outside filled the home that night just before a handful of adults and a dozen college students entered through the back door. As their smiles met mine, my habitual instinct to please people in a perfectly prepared home was replaced with a heightened desire to connect on a personal level. I found a spaciousness in my heart that I didn't know could exist.

Weeks later, I felt compelled to step outside on a sunny afternoon. I reverently stood still in God's presence as He opened my eyes to the beauty of clear, spacious skies, wide-open land, and an ever-expanding heart. With extended arms and falling tears, I worshipped God, the One who loosens the tightest of grips to make way for His glory.

—Cathy Baker

WHAT WILL YOU FIND?

Step outside beneath the spacious skies, confident God is there with you, and read Psalm 18:19 aloud. Prayerfully consider how God is loosening the grip of fears and ingrained habits in your life and introducing a greater spaciousness into your soul, freeing you to be who He created you to be.

In a Robin's Nest

"Look at the birds of the air; they do not sow or reap or store away in barns, and yet your heavenly Father feeds them. Are you not much more valuable than they?"
—MATTHEW 6:26 (NIV)

When a pair of robins began construction in the cedar shrub outside our kitchen window, I figured the only decent thing to do was stay out of the kitchen for a couple of months and give them their space. My husband, however, decided closing the Venetian blind between us and the nest would grant them all the privacy they required. Bummer.

But as the nest building process continued, I couldn't resist peeking in on the robins to see how they were doing. God spoke to my heart about the lessons I can learn from watching the birds at work.

Lesson One: Do the thing that lies within you to do. The robins were natural engineers, placing the twigs just so, then tamping them into place with their little feet. I couldn't build a nest like that without a kit of supplies, written instructions, and a whole lot of super glue. Even then, it would be shaped all wrong and probably fall apart in the first wind.

Robins, however, simply cannot fail at nest building. It's what they're hard-wired to do.

I believe God placed within each of us at least one thing we "can't not" do. Be it music, teaching, building, growing flowers—you name it—we know deep down we were created to do that activity. The difference between robins and humans is that we have a choice. We can abandon our purpose, and in the face of opposition, we often do.

But it's never too late to start again. The world needs your one thing, even when you're tired or discouraged enough to walk away. A half-built nest is worthless.

Lesson Two: Defend what you've been given to defend. Over the course of three days, Momma Robin laid three beautiful blue eggs and began the tenacious process of incubation. I knew there'd be no more opening the window to snap photos unless I wanted a close-up of a bird attack. Simply coming near the window earned me an instant open beak of warning. I wondered if she felt inclined to fly away instead, never to return.

What have you been called to protect and fight for? Family? The poor? The abused? Your gifts and talents? You may face attacks. The world doesn't always want the same thing you do. You may be tempted to step aside and surrender because it's easier. Please don't stop fighting when fighting is right.

Lesson Three: Hang on tight through the storms. When a massive windstorm hit our town, we watched from the safety of our house while the cedar bush by the kitchen window swayed and swirled. What would Momma Robin do? Could she hang on? Might she find a safer place? Would the nest come apart, dropping the eggs to the ground?

Though I can't imagine how fast her tiny heart must have been beating, she held firm. This chick knew her priorities.

We need to hang tough through the storms of life too, for they will come to all of us. Some bring more damage than others, but their threats seldom equal our fears. Morning eventually comes, bringing calm, sunshine, and hope.

That's a lot of education from such a small creature and her nest. All before the eggs even hatched! But throughout the process I felt God guiding me to watch and learn—and do my thing to share with others.

—*Terrie Todd*

WHAT WILL YOU FIND?

You don't need to go deep into nature to learn from God's creatures. Are there birds who live nearby, small animals who have adapted to living near human beings, or insects that have moved into your house or just outside? Next time you see one, pause and watch its behavior. What does it have to teach you?

Dancing in the Kitchen

But let all who take refuge in you be glad; let them ever sing for joy. Spread your protection over them, that those who love your name may rejoice in you.
—PSALM 5:11 (NIV)

Every surface of my kitchen was piled with something. Dirty pots and pans littered the stove, extra food was on trays, and something sticky spilled on the countertop. I had my work cut out for me. Unfortunately, it had been a long day, and cleaning the kitchen was the last thing I wanted to do.

I sighed, trying to decide where to begin. Then my daughter walked through the room. She was singing a song I remembered from my teen years, something fun and upbeat. I couldn't help but sing along as I opened the dishwasher. Hearing me join her, she promptly stopped and asked Alexa to play the song so we could start from the beginning together.

We started singing again (very off-key) and I asked her to grab some containers for the leftover food. She danced her way to the cabinet, and before I knew it, I was dancing a bit too. Just as the chorus peaked, we both started belting out the words with abandon, grinning ear to ear.

Singing and dancing, we cleaned a little and smiled a lot. Suddenly, I realized the mess around me wasn't dragging me down anymore, because I'd found joy in the middle of it. God had met me there, in the midst of my exhaustion, and sent my daughter to remind me to find the beauty in every moment. He was there in the mess and the joy, lifting both of us up, and building a memory that would carry us far into the future.

—*Rebecca Hastings*

WHAT WILL YOU FIND?

Head to your kitchen or another area needing some cleanup. Before you get started, play some fun music. Try singing or humming to the music, dancing, or something else that makes you smile. You can even ask someone to join you. As you tackle the mess, let the joy lift you.

On an Overstuffed Chaise

"My presence shall go with you, and I will give you rest."
—EXODUS 33:14 (NASB)

I know God is with me constantly and everywhere, for in the Bible He assures us He is with us always. But it's in my overstuffed chaise in my home study that I truly *feel* his presence. For nearly 20 years I've begun each morning there, coffee and Bible in hand, ensconced in blankets by the fireplace (regardless of season or temperature). This is my quiet time, a special time with God.

For thousands of hours, I've sat and talked with Him there. In that spot He has heard my prayers, pleas, cries, joys, laughter, longings, worship, and gratitude. In return, He has given me comfort, answers, guidance, and knowledge of his unfathomable love and peace.

Over the years this spot has become for me a sacred meeting place. It's in a room secluded from the rest of the house and filled with objects that hold a special meaning for me—mementos, books, Bibles, photographs, reminders of my goals and aspirations, little items that I especially love. Everything speaks of the incredible life God has blessed me with.

Above the fireplace is a painting of Jesus, head bowed. sitting in the wilderness. It reminds me that Jesus understands, that he too experienced wilderness, as we all do at times. I see Him listening, thinking, truly hearing what I pray.

In this quiet-time place I feel God's presence so strongly that wherever I go, if I ever feel tense, stressed, or anxious, all I need to do is go there in my mind, imagining myself in that spot, and I quickly feel the peace of His presence. It's a reminder that He is with me no matter where I go.

—*Kim Taylor Henry*

WHAT WILL YOU FIND?

Is there a place in your home where you can sit and absorb God's presence? If not, you can create one: Just find a place where you can close away the rest of the world, mentally if not physically, and just sit with God. Surround yourself with things that make you feel cozy and comfortable, and items that hold special meaning for you.

If you already have a special place, take a moment to close your eyes and transport yourself there mentally. What do you feel?

While Washing Dishes

First clean the inside of the cup and dish, and then the outside will also be clean.
—MATTHEW 23:26 (NIV)

I'm not ordinarily one to get excited over housecleaning. Picnics? Yes. Lunch with friends? A walk along the beach? Absolutely. But dusting, laundry, sweeping, or vacuuming? Not so much.

Washing dishes might be the exception to that rule. When I stand at a sudsy sink filled with dirtied dishes, soapy sponge in hand, the only thing required of me is to make sure the plates, glasses, cookware and flatware sparkle. Because washing dishes is such a simple task, my mind can indulge in the pleasure of floating along from one daydream to another, sharing the desires of my heart with God. With my thoughts cleared of day-to-day busyness, I find time to pray for loved ones, and for clarity as I consider personal challenges. But the most precious gift I receive during this task is the luxury of slowing down as my heart seeks and finds God. He's in the pretty dishes we use and the nutritious food I serve. His love warms my cozy kitchen, and my soul.

Sometimes, all it takes is a sink of dirty dishwater to make it crystal clear—He provides all the blessings that make up my life.

—*Heidi Gaul*

WHAT WILL YOU FIND?

As you clean your home, imagine clearing your mind of clutter as well. Acknowledge God's presence in even the simplest tasks as He pulls you closer, whispering of the ultimate security of His provision. Allow Him to replace your scattered thoughts with peace.

DEVOTION INDEX

Devotion titles are alphabetized by subject.

On an Answering Machine 108
In the Autumn Leaves 216
Wearing an Avon Calling Pin 192
In My Backyard 60
Holding an Autographed Baseball 11
Reading My Grandmother's Living Bible 94
Using a Bird ID App 152
Between the Blue Mountain Shadows 36
On a Boat at Night 40
At a Christian Bookstore 26
In a Yellow Butterfly 127
In a White Cardboard Box 168
Riding a Carousel 28
On an Overstuffed Chaise 244
Caring for Clara's Plant 46
Holding a Treasured Coffee Mug 233
In a Bag of Compost 159
In a Dog-Eared Cookbook 100
At the Corner with Walgreens and Family Dollar 76
In a Crossword Puzzle 214
In a Field of Daffodils 157
In the Dairy Aisle 202
Watching the Deer on the Wall 114
In the Desert, Under the Stars 200
Watching from Her Doorway 178

Looking Up at an Eclipse 144
Hearing an Elk Bugle 38
Holding Flashlight Batteries 72
While Restoring the Floor 208
At the End of the Fog 165
Staring into the Fog 66
On a Freeway North of Santa Barbara 161
Eating Fried Chicken and Biscuits 187
By a Front Door 229
As Gingko Leaves Fell 129
On Go-Home Day 227
Comforting My Anxious Goldendoodle 231
Singing "Great Is Thy Faithfulness" 96
On a Hay Bale 64
Putting Out a Help Wanted Sign 62
In a Prayed-For Home 24
Searching for Wild Horses 9
On a Hospital Lawn 74
In a Hospital Room at Night 78
Watching the Hummingbirds 163
On the Side of I-44 17
In a Jar of Salsa 13
In an Old Joke 204
Writing in My Daily Journal 196
Dancing in the Kitchen 242

In a Letter from a Sponsored Child   102
In a Hard Meeting   68
Talking to Mrs. Beasley   92
Holding My Sister's Nativity   104
Wearing a Nun's Habit   212
Underneath the Paragliders   52
In the Words on a Pendant   172
In a Stack of Pennies   185
Holding a Black-and-White Photo   98
In a Photo Album   176
At a Family Picnic   125
Sitting at the Pottery Wheel   118
In Grandma Currier's Quilt   120
In a Sudden Caribbean Rain   142
Following the Red Dirt Road   148
In a Redwood Tree Circle   85
My Grandma's Class Ring   189
Wearing My Mother's Ring   89
In the Ripples on the Water   123
On an Empty Road   218
In a Robin's Nest   239
In a Room Full of Mothers   50
In My Daddy's Rowboat   82
In My Scars   112
At a Security Checkpoint   70
In a Smiling Shadow   44
Swimming in Shark-Infested Waters   56

In Tiny Spiral Shells   154
In a Shoebox   15
Playing in the Snow   48
In a Social Media Memory   132
In a Spacious Place   237
In a Spider's Web   19
Holding a Red-Painted Spike   116
On an Old Staircase   235
Seeing a Statue of Jesus   138
In Dappled Sunlight   136
In the Sunlight on the Ocean   198
At an Ordinary Table   180
Sitting at the Roots Table   87
In the Ties that Bind   134
On a Mountain Trail   183
At the End of the Tunnel   32
On a Morning Walk through the Vineyard   150
Shopping in Walmart   22
While Washing Dishes   246
Wearing a Piece of a Platinum Watch   6
Beneath the Weeping Willow   220
Sailing Next to a Whale   210
Sitting in a Wing Chair   224
In a Stack of Wooden Blocks   174
At a Writing Retreat   42

DEVOTION INDEX

AUTHOR INDEX

Cathy Baker 66, 95, 129, 231, 237

Elsa Kok Colopy 127, 159, 198, 216

Laurie Davies 11, 32, 44, 174, 187

Kristy Dewberry 46, 92, 168

Shannon Due Dunlop 13

Heidi Gaul 29, 125, 218, 235, 246

Elly Gilbert 100, 112, 132, 202, 233

Lynne Hartke 9, 36, 52, 85, 123

Rebecca Hastings 50, 68, 78, 157, 242

Kim Taylor Henry 24, 89, 245

Jennie Ivey 19, 220

Linda L. Kruschke 104, 136, 148, 163

Vicki Kuyper 48, 154

Louis Lotz 98, 150, 196

Ericka Loynes 116, 229

Eryn Lynum 38, 70, 144, 165, 172, 183, 208

Roberta Messner 6, 62, 76, 87, 114, 134, 192, 224

Janet Newberry 181

Kate Rietema 64, 118, 138, 178

Lisa Saruga 204

Jenny Snow 22, 60, 96

Buck Storm 40, 56, 142, 161, 200, 210

Angela Ruth Strong 26, 42, 74, 227

Heather Tabers 17, 102

Terrie Todd 15, 120, 176, 185, 212, 239

Barbranda Lumpkins Walls 108

Jeannie Waters 73, 82, 152, 187, 214

ACKNOWLEDGMENTS

Every attempt has been made to credit the sources of copyrighted material used in this book. If any such acknowledgment has been inadvertently omitted or miscredited, receipt of such information would be appreciated.

Scripture quotations marked (CEV) are taken from *Holy Bible: Contemporary English Version*. Copyright © 1995 American Bible Society.

Scripture quotations marked (CSB) are taken from *The Christian Standard Bible*, copyright © 2017 by Holman Bible Publishers. Used by permission.

Scripture quotations marked (ESV) are taken from *The Holy Bible, English Standard Version*. Copyright © 2001 by Crossway Bibles, a division of Good News Publishers. Used by permission. All rights reserved.

Scripture quotations marked (KJV) are taken from the *King James Version of the Bible*.

Scripture quotations marked (MSG) are taken from *The Message*. Copyright © 1993, 2002, 2018 by Eugene H. Peterson.

Scripture quotations marked (NASB) are taken from the *New American Standard Bible®*, Copyright © 1960, 1971, 1977, 1995, 2020 by The Lockman Foundation. All rights reserved.

Scripture quotations marked (NCV) are taken from *The Holy Bible, New Century Version*. Copyright © 2005 by Thomas Nelson.

Scripture quotations marked (NIV) are taken from *The Holy Bible, New International Version®, NIV®*. Copyright © 1973, 1978, 1984, 2011 by Biblica, Inc. Used by permission. All rights reserved worldwide.

Scripture quotations marked (NKJV) are taken from the *New King James Version®*. Copyright © 1982 by Thomas Nelson. Used by permission. All rights reserved.

Scripture quotations marked (NLT) are taken from the *Holy Bible, New Living Translation*. Copyright © 1996, 2004, 2007, 2015 by Tyndale House Foundation. Used by permission of Tyndale House Publishers Inc., Carol Stream, Illinois. All rights reserved.

Scripture quotations marked (NRSVUE) are taken from the *New Revised Standard Version, Updated Edition*. Copyright © 2021 National Council of Churches of Christ in the United States of America. Used by permission. All rights reserved worldwide.

Scripture quotations marked (TLB) are taken from *The Living Bible*. Copyright © 1971 by Tyndale House Publishers, Inc., Carol Stream, Illinois. All rights reserved.

A NOTE FROM THE EDITORS

We hope you enjoyed *Where I Found God Today*, published by Guideposts. For more than 75 years, Guideposts, a nonprofit organization, has been driven by a vision of a world filled with hope. We aspire to be the voice of a trusted friend, a friend who makes you feel more hopeful and connected.

By making a purchase from Guideposts, you join our community in touching millions of lives, inspiring them to believe that all things are possible through faith, hope, and prayer. Your continued support allows us to provide uplifting resources to those in need. Whether through our communities, websites, apps, or publications, we inspire our audiences, bring them together, and comfort, uplift, entertain, and guide them. Visit us at guideposts.org to learn more.

We would love to hear from you. Write us at Guideposts, P.O. Box 5815, Harlan, Iowa 51593 or call us at (800) 932-2145. Did you love *Where I Found God Today*? Leave a review for this product on guideposts.org/shop. Your feedback helps others in our community find relevant products.

Find inspiration, find faith, find Guideposts.

Shop our best sellers and favorites at

guideposts.org/shop

Or scan the QR code to go directly to our Shop